ADVANCE PRAISE FOR *THE AGE OF PLURALISM*

'Here is a superb resource for any leader, executive or coach who wants to quickly rise to a new level of success in the complex and richly diverse business world of today and tomorrow.'

Marshall Goldsmith, *Thinkers 50* – World's Most Influential Leadership Thinker (two-time winner)

'If you want to succeed in the global marketplace, and to lead more collaborative, high performing teams at home and overseas, this is the book for you.'

John Mattone, the number one authority on Intelligent Leadership and the world's top executive coach

'This book is another gem from David Clive Price. It is both timely and insightful, with that special practitioner's touch. The world has changed and is changing ever faster. David recognizes this and empowers us to adapt and evolve to this new world, with the confidence that The Age of Pluralism provides us. David's own rich leadership journey through so many different cultures and environments is expertly retold in the most inclusive manner possible. A book for our times – not to be missed.'

René Carayol MBE, International Keynote Speaker, Author, and Leadership Guru.

'The Age of Pluralism is a highly engaging read for global companies, leaders and high-performing teams. Written with a rare combination of personal narrative, humour and 21-century tools for strengthening leadership agility, this is very much a book for our rapidly changing times. I would recommend it as essential reading for all current and emerging leaders as well as their coaches.'

Dr Thomas D. Zweifel, award-winning author of *Culture Clash 2: Managing the Global High-Performance Team*

'As somebody born in Argentina, who has lived in the USA and is now a British citizen, David's book strikes a chord. I consider myself both Argentine and British, and have embraced aspects of both cultures. In this sense, I'm a hybrid. In my leadership development work across the world, I see the pluralism David talks about manifested in how leaders navigate uncertainty, connect people and ideas, and deliver strategy through others. A very worthwhile read for any global citizen, senior leader or human resources leader who wants to go beyond diversity and cultural awareness.'

Mariano Tufro, Director, Leadership Minds Ltd.

'*The Age of Pluralism* goes directly to the heart of why current and emerging leaders fail to make the progress they want in our increasingly diverse world. The author provides deep insights into the challenges we face, and proposes practical and innovative solutions you can profit from for years to come.'

Tony J. Selimi, international number-one best-selling author of *A Path to Wisdom*

'The days of states in the global community existing within a singular cultural concept are long past. In the current framework of the global economy, we are becoming increasingly aware of the need to be more inclusive of the diversity that our global communities generate. Leadership as a whole is facing new challenges that past leadership did not encounter, at least not to the levels we are witnessing today.

The Age of Pluralism is a striking and timely reminder of the threats that exist for our emerging leaders. At the very moment when there is a clear and pressing need to prepare our leaders for the challenges of tomorrow, they find themselves seriously undervalued by senior leadership. David Clive Price showcases the reality facing our current leadership teams across the world. He explores the ever-present need for organisations to utilize the tools found in executive coaching to help their current emerging and high-potential leaders to succeed in positions of increasing seniority and responsibility.'

Curtis Smith, Founder & CEO, Thee Executive-Panel LLC

'In *The Age of Pluralism*, David Clive Price explores the increasing diversity of our times, and how we can harness the forces of pluralism to create more human centric leaders. By addressing the leadership gap between performance and coaching, David offers invaluable tools and resources as well as documented cases to accompany his personal, authentic narrative. A brilliant piece of work and highly relevant to today's global culture.'

Vivien Hunt, Leadership Coach and Director, Lead Source Coaching

'The Age of Pluralism distils a wealth of knowledge, real-life case studies and personal experiences from around the globe to produce an invaluable guide for both the next generation of future leaders and experienced executives alike.'

Grant Hall, Founder and CEO, League Cultural Diplomacy

'This is a must-read for any leader, executive or coach who wants to succeed during the next decade of increasing diversity, generational change and rapid innovation.'

Oleg Konovalov, bestselling author of *Corporate Superpower*

PRAISE FOR *BAMBOO STRONG*

'This book cuts to the chase as to why business owners and executives fail in new markets and cultures. It provides deep insights into the global challenges businesses face and delivers practical and innovative solutions you can profit from immediately. It's destined to be the cross-cultural handbook of the decade.'

Jason Jennings, worldwide bestselling author of *The High Speed Company, The Reinventors, Less Is More,* and *Think BIG—Act Small*

'An essential read that is a wise and powerful compendium of strategies to help you truly prosper as a business owner or executive in the new global economy. *Bamboo Strong* is about the most important problems arising today in the global economy, and it proposes strategies companies can implement now for a more fruitful tomorrow!'

Marshall Goldsmith, author of the #1 *New York Times* bestseller, *Triggers*

'A must-read for anyone who owns or manages a multicultural organisation or business and wants to create a culture of creativity and innovation based on diversity.'

John Mattone, the world's number one authority on Intelligent Leadership and top executive coach

'David is a very rare and special talent, and as with all those who were born to make a difference to our world, he openly shares his learning, insights, and experiences for our betterment. *Bamboo Strong* is a beautiful creation that is a book for the times we live in today and a guide for the world we would like to live in tomorrow. It challenged me and argued with me, made me laugh out loud, and made me weep with both joy and hurt. But, just like the bamboo in the title, it was supple enough to bend and accommodate my diversity and difference, and it was also strong enough to guide me when I wandered off near danger. A book for everyone and anyone you care about. An essential guide for the times we live in.'

René Carayol, MBE, CEO,
Inspired Leaders Network

'In his fascinating, beautifully written, and page-turning book, David helps you to uncover the essential skills you need to influence and inspire others who come from cultures that are not your own. In an era when the world has become a village and businesses of almost every kind operate in global markets, it has never been more important to acquire these lessons. Lean in to learn from a wonderful array of knowledge, expertise, and personal stories that will assuredly help you to chart a course to masterful cross-cultural communication.'

Eamonn O'Brien, founder of The
Reluctant Speakers Club and author of
How to Make Powerful Speeches

'This is the beautifully written and fascinating tale of David's journey to becoming a global citizen. Rather than boring you with classroom theory, you'll be enlightened and inspired to accompany him on his travels to embrace cultural intelligence so that you too can become a more effective leader in this new global world. For any business or organisation looking to forge profitable and peaceful partnerships across borders, I highly recommend you read this book and learn from David who is a visionary leader for the twenty-first century.'

Rachel Henke, International Freedom Coach
and bestselling author of *The Freedom Solution*

'With his invaluable insights and cultural intelligence practices, David has opened a new door for global business travelers. The *Bamboo Strong* mindset and David's newly designed dynamic activities are created to challenge thinking, encourage flexibility, and catalyze self-discovery. The flexible nature of this new guide is quintessentially bamboo: encouraging readers to nurture their own journey of self-discovery while cultivating the resilience to thrive in the complex circumstances and rich cultures of our time.'

Sharon Schweitzer, JD, President,
Protocol & Etiquette Worldwide, LLC,
and author of the *Access to Asia: Your
Multicultural Business Guides* series

'For anyone planning to engage with other countries, whether in business or out of a sense of adventure, this is an invaluable work. In today's fast moving and constantly changing world, *Bamboo Strong* provides the navigational chart to ensure smooth sailing in the complex waters of other cultures. It gives helpful insights through a rich array of anecdotes and stories to assist those seeking a greater understanding of sometimes seemingly confusing situations. An invaluable addition to anyone's armoury of cross-cultural knowledge!'

Roddy Gow, Chairman and founder, Asia Scotland Institute

'*Bamboo Strong* is a must-read for those who live in a culturally diversified environment, be it in the physical or online world. In this innovative and yet practical book, David educates and inspires readers with his authentic personal stories, third-party evidence and research, and a high CQ sense of humour that can resonate and connect with each of us, regardless of our skin colour and life experience. This is a great read for both business and leisure in the new global economy.'

Sally Maier-Yip, Managing Director, 11K Consulting

'*Bamboo Strong* should be essential reading for anyone hoping to be successful in business. The central message of this book is that unless you are open to the challenges of cultural intelligence (understanding the language within the language) you will not succeed. Bamboo is used as a good example of the need for malleability, as it has the ability to bend and accommodate in stressful conditions without losing its original shape. Recognizing that we live and work in a modern global village, companies are choosing to become matrix organisations and to embrace diversity as an opportunity in the search for talent. To win this talent race, an increasing number of successful companies are investing in understanding the implications of cultural intelligence.'

Mariano A. Davies, Former President and CEO, British Chamber of Commerce in Denmark

'Global executives need cross-cultural skills and intelligence now more than ever before. Success and the ability to outperform your competitors in international markets require sensitivity towards diverse local cultures and business etiquette. *Bamboo Strong* will guide you on this path, its gift being not only the enrichment of your business but also an enrichment of your life experience. A wonderful read packed with insights and examples to build awareness and provide the skills necessary to perform effectively across markets. This book will equip you to achieve a level of intercultural intelligence that is critical to long-term success in the global workplace. So take up the challenge and dive in!'

Catherine Lai, CEO, Albest International Limited

'Cultural intelligence is probably the most important skill required by today's leaders. In this masterful and incisive book, David demonstrates why and how to become more resilient and flexible, for greater success in cross-cultural relationships.'

Mindy Gibbins-Klein, MBA, international speaker and author of *The Thoughtful Leader*

'At long last, a book that explodes the myth that many businesses hold about culture being associated with optional skills on the peripheries of business but instead reveals how a high level of CQ impacts directly on profitability and performance for global businesses. Using personal experiences combined with proven academic studies, David celebrates the importance of cross-cultural effectiveness as a must-have skill for today's global managers, especially in today's evolving and multicultural world, where mastery of these skills can mean the difference between a project's success or failure.'

Sarah Parsons, Managing Director, Japan in Perspective

'The level of success in today's globalised commerce strongly depends on the cultural intelligence of leaders, which cannot be gained without sophisticated knowledge. *Bamboo Strong* explains this complex phenomenon in a very classy, elegant, and practical manner.'

Dr Oleg Konovalov, DBA, MBA, author of *Organisational Anatomy*

'You are at the center of the global experience. How can you become a Bamboo Leader? You will need your own copy of *Bamboo Strong* to understand the analogy. You will also need to be open to the experience and ready to travel. You will want to discover and develop that part of your brain (or heart) that is like your cultural muscle. *Bamboo Strong* is not a list of facts or behaviours that are acceptable or best avoided. It is a very personal and experiential book about life, courage, and resilience. It raises awareness of cultural intelligence and introduces new ways of looking at diversity, so that we can all identify and think of our own circumstances and stories.'

Sophie Leroi, Executive and Global Leadership Coach, founder, The Focus Room, LLC

'We are crossing borders and bridging worlds now faster than ever before. This timely book is a powerful tool that lets us ride on the evolutionary wave towards becoming a flexible Bamboo Leader and bridges the separations that we see outside ourselves so we can do better business. David guides us to work with our inner separations, which are at the root of almost all the pains and problems we experience in daily life. This is a book with a heart and sense of balance that I consider rare at this level of business books. David's message helps us lower our own barriers to become more responsive, share, grow, and profit together.'

Adam Frewer, global healer, channel, and author of *From Baggage to Balance*

THE AGE OF
PLURALISM

GLOBAL INTELLIGENCE
FOR EMERGING LEADERS

DAVID CLIVE PRICE

WILDBLUE
PRESS

WildBluePress.com

THE AGE OF PLURALISM published by:

WILDBLUE PRESS
P.O. Box 102440
Denver, Colorado 80250

WILDBLUE PRESS is registered at the U.S. Patent and Trademark Offices.

ISBN 978-1-948239-94-3   Trade Paperback
ISBN 978-1-948239-95-0   eBook

Interior Formatting/Book Cover Design by Elijah Toten
www.totencreative.com

THE AGE OF
PLURALISM

GLOBAL INTELLIGENCE
FOR EMERGING LEADERS

ALSO BY DAVID CLIVE PRICE

Alphabet City, a novel

*Bamboo Strong: Cultural Intelligence Secrets
to Succeed in the New Global Economy*

Buddhism: The Fabric of Life in Asia

Chinese Walls, a novel

Phoenix Rising: A Journey through South Korea

The Master Key to Asia

The Master Key to China

The Other Italy

Travels in Japan

For Simon Chu, Shiu Ming
My fellow amphibian
With love and gratitude

'Pluralism isn't just diversity; it's something we create out of this diversity.'

Diana L. Eck

'Pluralism is no longer simply an asset or a prerequisite for progress and development, it is vital to our existence.'

Aga Khan IV

CONTENTS

FOREWORD

In today's business world, the rate of change is at an all-time high. Rapid digitization and globalisation the likes of which we have never seen before are transforming the face of global business and making the competitive environment far more unpredictable than it was even a decade ago. Changes are sweeping business today—VUCA pressures, digital disruption, increased connectivity, demographics, migration. Indeed, there is nowhere to hide.

Leaders must be agile, resilient, and responsive just to keep up. Teams are working under greater pressure. High potential and emerging leaders need to be identified and developed earlier and more effectively. But as David reveals in this book, leaders already have the capability to handle change and complexity from within themselves.

In the Age of Pluralism, our backgrounds, work, and life experiences are becoming increasingly intermingled and heterogeneous. Leaders need to embrace and leverage these differences in order to succeed. Rather than expect everyone to be just like themselves, they must look within and see things from different perspectives. They must put themselves in the place of others and have the courage to go outside their comfort zones.

As a CEO coach, I have long recognized that most learning for leaders happens through self-discovery and the involvement and input of stakeholders and mentors. This reinforces the value of introspection and making the decision to be vulnerable, and therefore open to the views and feedback of others.

In this powerful book, David shows us that the 'vulnerable' future is already upon us: more open and connected societies, more outreach, and more resilient and responsive leaders. At the very heart of the book, David provides a 'global leadership toolkit': three essential tools for becoming stronger leaders able to shine on a global platform.

If you want to succeed in the global marketplace, and to lead more collaborative, high performing teams at home and overseas, this is the book for you.

John Mattone, the #1 authority on Intelligent Leadership and the world's top executive coach

ACKNOWLEDGEMENTS

I am very grateful to my extraordinary clients, readers, online community, friends, and 'amphibians' in many countries and cultures that gave me the inspiration to write *The Age of Pluralism*. Their readiness to explore and leverage diversity, and to help others become more agile and inclusive leaders, gave me the vision for this book. They know who they are, and I thank them for their example, encouragement and friendship.

I'd like to thank Michael Cordova and his team at WildBlue Press for supporting me through the creative stages of this book and helping me deliver its systems and teachings to the world.

I'd also like to thank Csaba Toth of ICQ Consulting, Curtis Smith of Thee Executive-Panel, Dr Terence Jackson of Jackson Consulting Group, Dr Thomas D. Zweifel for the inspiration of his book *Culture Clash 2*, Dr David Streiff for his generous support, John Mattone of John Mattone Global, Lori Harris of Agape Consulting, Mariano Tufro of Leadership Minds, Dr Oleg Konovalov of Valuekod, Vivien Hunt of LeadSource Coaching, Karin Volo of Evoloshen Academy, Warwick John Fahy of Ashridge Executive Education, and my fellow Intelligent Leadership coaches for their invaluable support and advice.

And finally I'd like to thank my loyal, supportive husband, Simon, who continues to help me swim not sink, and who has always supported my mission to make the world a better place. I love and treasure you.

AUTHOR'S NOTE

We are living in an extraordinary age in which pluralism has become a major part of our lives, and is set to become an even greater force for change and human development in the decades to come. Under the impact of technological advances, super connectivity, mobility of talent, changing migration patterns, and the sheer diversity of our global knowledge and experiences, the peoples of the world have become more plural than ever before in human history.

Pluralism means that our backgrounds—especially those of our young people—are far more heterogeneous than might have been expected from previous categorisations by nationality, culture, race or religion. This is not simply multiculturalism as defined by the 'identity and values' versus 'globalisation and elites' movements of our times. Pluralism is not a movement. It is a fact of life—and it is the future.

As people travel more from their home of origin, intermarry more, study in more regions of their own country or in foreign countries, work in more far-flung international and virtual teams, connect with other cultures and cities, and experiment with lifestyles and viewpoints they would never have attempted before, they are coming to regard their ability to be plural or hybrid as a thrilling adventure, a lifetime's calling.

However, there are counter-currents and obstacles along the way. Every revolution produces a counter-revolution.

According to many commentators and politicians, this is what we are experiencing now.

We are living in an era of populism—at least in the politics of the West. There is no shortage of tub-thumpers and demagogues warning us of the dangers of globalisation, of the people and communities that have been left behind, of the threats of multiculturalism and unchecked immigration to fragmenting societies. The emphasis of populism and nativism is on barriers, not bridges; on protecting national identity and values; on defending the monoculture from immigrant invasion. Populists move quickly from inciting fears over cultural disintegration to complaining bitterly about diversity and liberalism, as if these drivers of world progress could somehow be put back into the bottle. But in fact the genie has long escaped from the bottle.

The old assumptions about 'pure' monocultures are fast becoming defunct. Not only is it impossible to consider people as simply representatives of their culture, the once governing cultures are themselves becoming fragmented, kaleidoscopic, intermingled and thrillingly complex. The hectic pace of technological change is driving this diversity. Soon there will be four billion Internet users in the world, and more of them will be speaking Mandarin than English.

It's the same story in the United States, with the number of Spanish speakers (and voters) rapidly growing. Spanish is the second most dominant language in the country after English. It is spoken by almost 50 million people, and census data suggests that by 2060 the Latinx population—the group most likely to speak Spanish—will grow some 115 per cent to 119 million. The Hispanic population in the United States is already the fifth largest in the world. There are similarly diverse populations in Australia, Canada, the Netherlands,

France, Germany, and United Kingdom, to name just a few countries. Indeed, defining a country by a single culture or even a predominant culture is fast becoming obsolete. The supposedly monolithic India has more than 100 spoken languages and more than 200 mother tongues. Indonesia, with the world's fourth largest population, has more than 700 different languages.

However, it's not only racial and linguistic diversity that is a fact of life. It's the diversity of generations, genders, ethnicities, cultures, educational levels, and above all generations, in our interconnected societies and businesses. Senior executives and CEOs at multinational companies are increasingly diverse, and they come from backgrounds that are neither exclusively white nor exclusively male. Similarly, the experience of millennials or Generation Y (aged 20-34) and of Generation X (aged 34-54) is almost entirely hybrid, made up of crosscutting cultural dynamics that have influenced them ever since they were born. These dynamics fuel a much greater need to be involved in the world and make a global impact than ever before.

Such are the visions driving the emerging leaders of the future, the high potentials who are seeking to gain more influence in their organisations and who are ready to step up to assume greater responsibility as the traditional concept of the hierarchical organisation breaks down. Many are being relocated or are already living and working in the dynamic emerging economies, such as those of China, India, Malaysia, Mexico, and Turkey.

These emerging leaders are increasingly well travelled, knowledge- and information-rich, high tech, and social media savvy, used to disruptive innovations, cosmopolitan in tastes and outlook, and able to thrive in new cultural situations.

But there is one area of the modern world where they are still lacking—*leadership*. In order to truly flourish as leaders of the future, these younger generation entrepreneurs and executives need more than an ability to succeed in new environments. To be strong and responsive leaders of diverse teams, cultural agility is no longer enough. Leaders must also identify their inner weaknesses and ignite their inner strengths. They must leverage personal *as well as* cultural differences to gain trust and build collaborative relationships in their home workplace, across borders and globally. In order to influence character, they must know their own character. All the more surprising, therefore, that so little is being done to develop these traits.

According to the Global Leadership Forecast, a survey of a thousand C-level executives worldwide(1), only 14 per cent of CEOs believe they have the leadership talent to execute their upcoming strategy. Among the Top Ten challenges listed, 64 per cent of C-Level executives identified the development of Next Generation leaders, 60 per cent indicated a failure to attract or retain top talent, and 48 per cent pointed to new global competitors. A stunning 78 per cent of human resources professionals considered their organisation's leadership planning systems to be only moderately effective or worse.

So at a time when organisations need more leaders— caused by the single largest departure of leaders in modern history—organisations are facing a shortfall in planning and leadership experience.

---

1.   2018. Published by Development Dimensions International and the Conference Board

Recent research shows that only 52 per cent of millennials feel prepared to take on their new roles. Given that frontline leaders play such a crucial part in the near-term implementation and execution of business strategy, these gaps can only have serious negative impacts on long-term growth. Millennials are estimated to number some 78 million in America alone. The global population of emerging leaders is exponentially greater, and is now ready to reshape the world's economy. So what is being done to equip them?

Many organisations use executive coaching to address leadership challenges. Executive coaching is a $1.5 billion per year industry, with most of the biggest enterprises now using coaches. The numbers continue to increase. Industry surveys suggest there are 25,000+ business coaches in Europe, which comprises about 40 per cent of all business coaches in the world (estimated at 150,000+).

However, while executive coaching is top-of-mind for executives and human resources, further research shows that only 35 per cent of global organisations used executive coaching for their emerging leaders(2). By contrast, 48 per cent of the organisations use executive coaching for VP level and senior executives, while 65 per cent of the organisations surveyed do not consider executive coaching an important developmental strategy for their high-potential pipeline. This shortfall represents a significant opportunity for organisations and coaches—especially in light of what different generations expect from their employers.

In many studies, Generation X employees reveal they want a casual, independent, flexible environment, and a place to learn; Generation Y employees want a structured,

2. Trends in Executive Development Research Study (Pearson)

supportive, and interactive environment. Both want continuous growth and 'connectedness' with people—including people they interact with throughout the world.

In the following chapters, I offer a clear and actionable process to help create stronger leaders for today's multi-dimensional and multi-polar business world. My intention is to speak personally and directly from my own experiences and those of my clients, colleagues, and partners in many different work and life situations around the world.

In Part One, I guide you through the challenges to global leadership presented by populist, nativist, and tribalist movements in many countries. I also look at the false dichotomy between diversity and opposition to immigration. In Part Two, I provide three specific tools for global leadership: the Bamboo Strong™ CQ Model for developing cultural intelligence; the Global DISC™ assessment for leveraging personal and cultural differences; and Intelligent Leadership™, an immersive leadership development experience founded by world-leading executive coach John Mattone.

In Part Three, I explore the importance of 'connectedness' and moving beyond diversity into the future—one that is already upon us and all around us. Throughout this book, I offer unique solutions for developing current and emerging global leaders while showing you the skill sets and coaching solutions you need to collaborate with people of different personalities, genders, backgrounds, generations, and cultures. To this end, in the Postscript, I include a number of action steps, boot camps, resources, and checklists to create your own strategy for becoming Bamboo Global Leaders.

Please let me know about your global leadership experiences. You can connect with me by registering for the

Age of Pluralism Planner and by joining my email subscriber list: **http://davidcliveprice.com/planner**

You can also reach out to me on social media and read about my global leadership strategies at **http://www.davidcliveprice.com**.

To your global leadership success!

Dr David Clive Price, Global Executive Coach,
International bestselling author of *Bamboo Strong*

PART ONE

*

THE CHALLENGE FOR GLOBAL LEADERSHIP

1. TRIBAL TOM-TOMS

Tribalism: a very strong feeling of loyalty to a political or social group, so that you support them whatever they do (Cambridge Dictionary)

I was sitting in the coffee bar of my local gym the day after the wedding of Meghan Markle to Prince Harry and discussing the wedding coverage in the newspapers with Dev, a member of my gym class.

Dev is of Indian descent but he has lived all his life in London, and he works for a big legal firm as a strategic advisor.

'It's all a bit overblown,' said Dev. 'I mean, yes, she has a black mother and a white father, but it's not as if racial discrimination is going to die out overnight just because they've got hitched.'

'No', I said, 'that's very true. But the media have painted it as a symbol of changing times—and I have to say they have a point.'

Dev looked at me quizzically, as if I didn't quite understand the issues at stake. Then he smiled. 'Something tells me you are a true Brit—queen and country and all that. A bit of a royalist?'

I laughed. It was true I did have a sneaking admiration for things royal, history, and traditions, ever since I was a boy. I rather liked pomp and ceremony, at least the way Brits did them (and the French too), and I had studied kings and queens and courts for my history degree.

So yes, I had enjoyed the Royal Wedding—but just as much for what it represented as for what actually took place. It didn't move me because it was royal and British and confirmed my tribal identity.

It moved me because it was interracial and celebratory of mixed heritage. There was a black gospel choir from London singing the spiritual 'This Little Light of Mine'. There was a rousing, evangelist-style sermon from a senior American black bishop, quoting Martin Luther King Jr. There was young, award-winning black cellist Sheku Kanneh-Mason playing Fauré.

And most of all, there was an American actress bride of mixed heritage supported by her cool and elegant mother Doria. And all this within St. George's Chapel at Windsor Castle, attended by the cream of the British establishment.

'But it's not just me, Dev. I think a lot of people liked it, not because it celebrated Britishness. But because the mixed race thing was no big deal. It was kind of, well, normal.'

'Mmmm,' said Dev. 'Let's see how that pans out. One mixed race royal marriage is not going to solve racial discrimination all in one go. People are still going to stick to their tribes.'

'That's true,' I said. 'But most people were more interested in her dress and outfits than her skin colour—isn't that a sign of progress? I mean, maybe we're starting to grow up. Maybe we're ready to stop defining people simply by what they look like.'

'Or by the tribes they belong to,' said Dev and took a long meaningful sip of his coffee.

In the following days I thought a lot about Dev and that comment about tribes. And I did some research.

It turned out that he was right. According to Trevor Phillips, former chairman of the UK Equality and Human Rights Commission, Britain is now the western country in which interracial marriages are most common. There are more than 1 million dual-heritage Brits, the largest single group being the children of white Brits and people of African or Caribbean descent. By 2030, if the term 'black British' is ever used, it is more likely to mean mixed race. The usual tribal epithets will become irrelevant.

So maybe I was right too. The wedding of Prince Harry and Meghan Markle showed that mixed-race marriages aren't exceptional. Indeed, the problem with dividing the world into tribes is that it leaves out these essential drivers of modern life. In a unique way, the children of mixed marriages combine two different worlds, increasingly at ease in all parts of society rather than being identified by their skin colour or tribe.

We are not defined by simple labels or movements or assumed loyalties. We are not one thing or another. Whatever the politicians and social media and pundits might say, we are not black and white, not even physically. And we cannot hope to influence, guide, and collaborate with other people— especially in our incredibly interconnected world—if we rely on tribal allegiances and readymade categories.

Today's global economy is far too fast moving and fluid to be divided into tribes. However much populist movements and protectionists, nationalists, and nativists try to divide the world based on identity— into tribes of 'them' and 'us', countries and groups, races and religions, local and global— they cannot hold back the tide of pluralism that is sweeping the globe.

And in order to ride this wave, leaders must be able to embrace complexity and change, reach out to other viewpoints and perspectives, and learn to create new combinations and richer amalgams of thought and action.

Most commentators misunderstand the nature of tribes. Their view of them as primitive and insular, even violent, is common in the vocabulary of modern politics. It's as if the recourse to tribalism is some ancient mechanism, a return to an ancestral way of doing things. In our vague anthropology, we think of tribes as imposing unity on individuals by repetitive social customs. Contemporary tribes such as political parties are seen as a natural refuge from inevitable conflict. They are exclusionary and conformist, offering safety in numbers and an admiration of authoritarianism. They believe in their moral superiority.

But as many anthropological studies show, actual tribes are characterized by surprisingly open boundaries.(3) They experiment with other tribes' practices and social forms. They frequently adopt outsiders. Captured white settlers were often invited into the communal life of North American tribes (even staying in the group when liberated). Among certain tribes in North Africa, members can voluntarily leave their own tribe and join another.

Traditional tribesmen continually create forms of mutual obligation, not only within the tribe but also across tribes. Leaders of the Berbers of North Africa, for example, are commonly chosen or ratified by the group's opponents in the belief that one's current enemy may later be an ally.

Imagine the Republicans and Democrats in the USA choosing the other party's leaders! What would happen if

3. Lawrence Rosen, A Liberal Defence of Tribalism, Foreign Policy 2018

members of the populist right wing and left wing parties of Europe changed loyalties every so often? Many tribes, such as the Mae Enga of Papua New Guinea and the Lozi of Central Africa, even share the practice of marrying members of enemy tribes to reduce the possibility of inter-tribal warfare. Grandchildren are raised in different kinship groups, and a majority of tribes are multilingual due to intermarriage and strong trading relations.

Tribes do not need to be exclusionary to flourish. You might draw parallels with contemporary educational exchange between countries like China and the USA, or the incubator startups and digital entrepreneurs of Bangalore or Silicon Valley or Shanghai. These open groups are much more like traditional tribes in the sense of being built on the cross-fertilization of ideas. They are inherently non-authoritarian, inclusive, and loosely democratic.

The partisan tribes of our contemporary politics are mainly characterized by aggression and, above all, a sense of moral superiority. This is in direct contrast to historical tribes. Most of these groups, as the anthropologist Paul Dresch says of Yemeni tribes, practice an 'avoidance of any absolute judgment, a kind of moral particularism or pluralism.' This is because traditional tribes know that social isolation or claims of moral superiority limit their flexibility. They must be able to adapt to survive. They cannot adapt if they are exclusive, or if they have a rigid set of rules for every situation.

Present day identity politics borrows the warring images of tribes to make our politics much more adversarial than necessary. It seals tribal members off from other tribes and, more damagingly, from the diversity and accelerating technological change that is the reality for thousands of intermingling cultures across the globe. Rather than cutting people off from each other and seeking security in smaller groups—as our current political tribes attempt—we should be embracing the opportunities of collaboration, innovation, and creativity that the global economy presents.

Whether we like it or not, we are now more interconnected than ever before, and we have far less scope for thinking of people far away as 'not like us' or worse, 'stupid'. All the peoples of the world are teaching each other new perspectives, different visions, unexpected connections on a daily basis. You may think of yourself a being part of the post-globalisation wave. You may consider yourself a member of a tribe that has been left behind by the rising tide of globalisation. You may even be anti-globalist.

It doesn't matter. Whether your tribe is for or against globalisation, we are all global citizens now. Rather than seeing the world in terms of tribal or nationalist loyalties, it is much more productive—and tribal in the traditional sense—to think of yourself as a global citizen.

This does not mean that you are a 'citizen of nowhere', as British prime minster Theresa May once declared in relation to international business élites. It does mean that you are plugged into the cultures, perspectives, and customs of people of many backgrounds all across the world. You may be following them on the Internet or via streaming devices. You may be doing business with them. They may be part of your international or virtual team. They may be just round the corner or at the farthest end of the globe. You may access them via translation apps, or simply in the lingua franca of English, Spanish, or Chinese via Skype or Zoom.

However you relate to them, they are part of your daily world and business life. Thinking in purely 'tribal' terms means that you are almost certainly missing out on vast areas of experience and abundance that this extraordinary wired planet of ours now offers. Get over the old tribalism—which is, in fact, a caricature of tribalism. Become a leader in the borderless world that is now at your fingertips!

The leaders of the future must look beyond tribes and borders. They must cultivate an inner curiosity and malleability to thrive in many different cultural situations, and with people of many different backgrounds. When Berber tribes find themselves in a dispute, one group may call on the leader of the other to settle the claim, in the knowledge that he will not risk his ability to form later alliances by supporting his own side.

Now that's what I call global leadership.

2. THE RISE OF THE AMPHIBIANS

Looking back, I guess I always thought of myself as a bit of an amphibian. In every place and culture I went, I sank or swam—and usually swam.

According to the dictionary, the literal definition of *amphibian* is 'a cold-blooded vertebrate animal of a class that comprises the frogs, toads, newts, salamanders, and caecilians. They are distinguished by having an aquatic gill-breathing larval stage followed typically by a terrestrial lung-breathing adult stage.'

I am not cold blooded (I hope), nor have I moved from breathing through gills to breathing through lungs. But the broader sense of the word, derived from the Greek word *amphibious*, suggests having two lives or living in both water and on land. This is borne out by the modern adaptation of the noun 'amphibian', meaning a vehicle that is able to move on both land and water, or an aeroplane that can land on both land and water.

So my metaphor of sinking or swimming is reasonably accurate. My parents were born in Wales but I was born in London, so nothing very exotic there. Perhaps I first learned to sink or swim as a 17-year-old grammar school boy going up to Cambridge University, where I found myself surrounded by more mature public school boys. They already had cosmopolitan airs and had the money to travel in their summer vacations.

It was only when I was well into my postgraduate studies that I met my first partner, who happened to be Swiss German. So on finishing my doctorate, I made a big decision. I went to live with Davide and his family in Switzerland—which is when my amphibian instincts took over. I learned Swiss German to converse with my family while I also improved my French. Under the influence of the Swiss *Sprachwunder* (language miracles) all around me, I also learned rudimentary Italian and helped Davide organize a film festival every year in Locarno, in the Italian part of Switzerland.

From Locarno it seemed just a short step into Italy itself. I was lucky. I managed to obtain a British Academy Travel Fellowship at the University of Bologna, and then went on to lecture on Renaissance history at the European Institute in Florence. Nothing seemed to stop me exploring at that age. Nothing seems to stop young people now, who are, if anything, more *amphibious* than me. I lived for a while in a converted garage near Bologna station (convenient for trains to the archives in Modena and Mantua). And then together with Davide, I bought a broken-down farmhouse in Tuscany and for a while, I commuted to Florence, while I worked the land for wine and olives, Davide commuted to Locarno, and I began to write my first novel.

It all seemed to happen naturally somehow. One moment I was studying in the cloistered halls of Cambridge University and the next I was a farmer and writer in Italy. And it didn't end there. In order to research that first novel, I eventually decided to take a year off from Tuscany and travel to New York. There I rented a cheap apartment just south of the downtown area of Manhattan called Alphabet City (Avenues A to C). At that time in the early 1980s, the streets to the south of East Houston Street were not entirely safe, but they hosted a richly diverse and not-yet-gentrified sub-culture in which citizens of every race and nation on Earth were gathered in close proximity. Rich terrain to set a novel.

Indeed, New York gave me confidence to celebrate being *amphibious*, while also giving me the freedom to be creative alongside people from many different backgrounds— Jews, blacks, Hispanics, Eastern Europeans, Chinese, Koreans— who I met there and who seemed to be as *amphibious* as I was. Perhaps it was no surprise that I met and fell in love with an African American painter while I lived in Alphabet City. My passion was not reciprocated and by the time I returned to Italy, my decade-long relationship with Davide was seriously damaged. It took us another two years to split. I stayed on at the farm to write my book and then Davide encouraged me to seek new pastures in a region of the world that was already fascinating me.

Instead of returning to England, I headed for Tokyo. And then, after a year of finding that I was more sinking than swimming, I followed Davide's generous advice and moved to Hong Kong.

Arriving in this British colony with nothing much more than a PhD and a couple of published books in my luggage, I found work as a economics researcher for the Economist Intelligence Unit. After a couple of years finding my feet, I successfully applied for the position of speechwriter for HSBC, one of the world's leading banks. My remit was to create the key messages for the handover of Hong to China in July 1997. I also met Simon, a young Hong Kong Chinese man who was in a group of friends who came to the airport to greet me on my arrival from Tokyo. I have been together with him ever since.

So yes, I became an Asian amphibian. In order to explore my new family and their culture, I lived together with Simon's mother, sister, and nephew in their small apartment in a Kowloon housing estate. In that way I really got to know about Chinese daily life, festivals, and customs, even as I took a taxi each morning to work in the shiny HSBC headquarters in the Central financial district.

One of the big benefits of being in a multinational was that I could continue my work as a freelance writer in my spare time and long vacations. So I travelled extensively in South Korea, Japan, Myanmar, China, Thailand, all the while writing books and articles. Throughout this period I also continued to adopt the same *amphibious* approach as I had in Europe: Swim, David! Don't sink!

Indeed, I have continued to live like this ever since: being ready to explore in a new culture, having one foot here and one foot there, getting adopted by locals or even a whole family. In so doing, I have often found myself an outsider, on the edge of a culture where I can communicate both ways— into and out of the group. But whereas I once thought I was one of a lucky few who sought out these hybrid experiences, now I think it is quite commonplace.

This is especially true of the young leaders and potential leaders of today. It's amazing how many millennials now seem to be of mixed background. I've lost count of the number of people who tell me they are Third Culture Kids or TCKs. This term, first used by sociologist Ruth Hill Useem in the 1950s for children raised in a culture other than their parents' (or the culture of a country given on a child's passport), has become a mark of pride for many people of mixed parentage.

I was recently coaching an executive who was brought up in his father's native country of Brazil. He speaks Portuguese and English, but currently lives in California near his mother, managing two trading teams in Singapore and Malaysia. He calls himself a TCK and was rather aggrieved that he wasn't getting the results he deserved from his Southeast Asia teams, 'even though I am used to adapting to other cultures.'

I have another colleague, Eric, who is married to a Japanese woman, but who spent several years in Shanghai and has a Chinese mother and a French father. He speaks Mandarin, French, and English, and now lives and works in London and New York. His children speak English, French, and Mandarin. Perhaps unsurprisingly, he is an expert in international start-ups.

This amphibiousness seems to have become more marked as the pace of technological change, international travel, interracial marriage, matrix working, and social media quickens. Not only is everyone connected, but also several life experiences are connected within one person or one family.

Amphibians are pluralism personified. However, pluralism isn't just living with difference, or tolerating difference, or even celebrating difference. It's discovering that you have roots here but also there, a dynamic that creates a third personality. 'Being hyphenated can sometimes cause problems,' one TCK told me. 'But it's also fun.'

I am not officially hyphenated but my hybrid experiences have made a coherent identity of all my influences. Of course it might not be so much fun for others, such as expatriate executives, who are sometimes relocated time and again because they haven't been able to work in the prevailing culture.

I can think of many people in the multinationals where I've worked, or executive clients who have been discomfited by new cultural situations, new members of their international teams, or new in-country assignments where they simply have not 'gelled'. Failing in Japan or Saudi Arabia or Mexico (or on the East and West Coasts of the US) costs companies huge amounts of money in replacement costs and also in repatriating disgruntled executives, who may well leave the company in the aftermath of disappointment.

Research shows that some 65 per cent of expatriates fail in the first or second posting, while 90 per cent of global executives identify cross-cultural effectiveness as their biggest challenge.(4)

Clearly, there are many professionals out there who are non-amphibians. However, the more you look around the more you see examples of interesting and hybrid backgrounds, especially among the often well-travelled and footloose younger generation. These are our future leaders. And although they may not be ready for leadership yet, many of them are already tending towards that edge-of-the-group mindset and appreciation of mixed influences where creativity flourishes. If you look at Western media, TV, and films—or even Japanese, Korean, or Latin American media and films—you will see mixed race, mixed sexuality, and mixed backgrounds portrayed on the screen now far more than ever before.

---

4. Soon Ang, Linn van Dyne and M.L. Tan, "Cultural Intelligence" in *Cambridge Handbook of Intelligence* (CUP 2013)

Our *Master Chef* and *Celebrity Bake-off* programmes on UK television are full of exotic 'fusion' dishes from cuisines all over the world. The contestants are British-born Somalis and Nigerians, Indians, Chinese, Sri Lankans, Columbians, Cypriots, Italians, and many others of diverse backgrounds. It's perhaps no surprise that it is these contestants who are often the most creative.

But what really makes an amphibian succeed? What makes one person flourish in diverse situations and cultures, some of them far removed from anything they have experienced before, while another is like a fish out of water? What are the main drivers that are making the amphibians thrive with every fresh experience of difference?

3. BRIDGES NOT BARRIERS

If we can identify what makes amphibians succeed, we are halfway to reproducing those special qualities in our leaders. Amphibians not only have the ability to bring people together within communities, they also have the qualities to create bridges between communities. Rather than focusing on what divides us, on walls and exclusion and intolerance, they create synergies through openness and communication.

The defining trait of amphibians is that they come to regard their ability to explore other cultures and backgrounds as a great adventure, something they could not live without. They make bridging to others a daily challenge and mission. If we could bottle their adventurousness, it would become an elixir for current and emerging leaders everywhere.

Having grown up with technology, the millennial 'digital natives' also see travelling and living outside their native lands as completely natural. Surveys show that many undergraduates are extremely keen to work abroad in the early part of their careers. However, despite mass travel and interest in different countries, adapting to new cultures and speaking foreign languages are still barriers to employees wanting to work abroad.

A research report by *Going Global* found that only one in five human resources managers rated the geographic mobility of their young employees as strong.(5) The majority thought there is more work that new hires can do to

5. Going Global Research Report 2018

develop the skills or self-confidence to work internationally. Nearly two-thirds of hiring executives recommended that working outside comfort zones was a key driver for both new hires and emerging leaders, with just a third saying that taking on international assignments helped boost the career growth of high potential professionals.

In other words, the majority of emerging leaders do not yet have an amphibian mindset. This is particularly important in the context of cross-border management in matrix organisations. According to a CEMS Global Alliance report on 30 business schools across five continents, aspiring global leaders need to up-skill in six significant areas: change agility, cross-cultural sensitivity, managing diversity, networking, integrity and compliance, and innovation.

There is no doubt that the seasoned amphibians can show the way to emerging leaders in these areas, helping them to build bridges into new business worlds and different mindsets.

Looking back on my own experiences, as well as those of my colleagues and clients in many countries and organisations, I offer the following Global Leadership Checklist for current and emerging leaders:

1. Curiosity

You have to forget knowing the answers to everything, as well as your ready-made stereotypes, and instead get excited about new situations or relationships that you may never have experienced before. You have to really *want* to know. Falling in love with an 'other' person helps, but failing that, you need to be constantly wondering what makes another person tick, what is different in their background, what is going on in their unfamiliar approach to a familiar situation.

It's so very easy to assume you know everything. Having an open and inquisitive mind will soon tell you that you don't. The more you achieve this viewpoint, the stronger your curiosity will become in every new situation. This is an essential leadership skill in today's global economy.

2.   Listening and observing

It's easy to assume that with your level of knowledge and expertise, people in other companies, countries, and cultures will want to hear from you. They won't. They will only listen to you (eventually) if you are not talking but spending a lot of time getting on the same wavelength as them. That means a LOT of listening and observing. Think of yourself as a spy, a cultural 007. In any new environment, you don't know what the codes are, what the needs are, what the customs, and respect systems are. If you just try to bluff your way through, you will be ignored—and also disliked. Every attempt you make to suggest (or worse, impose) changes will be met with resistance. Don't go at it like a bull in a china shop. Stand back, ask questions, and make few comments. That will help you to swim not sink.

3.   Sense of humour in awkward circumstances

I can think of no more dependable creator of productive relationships than a sense of humour. I don't mean telling jokes in your mother tongue, which often fall embarrassingly flat and are not appreciated. I mean knowing how to defuse an awkward situation where you aren't acquainted with the usual behaviour or customs. Simply smiling or making a comment through body language often helps break the ice. Body language is a great vehicle for humour—and it has the added benefit that you are not trying to impose yourself through talking. Little gestures, such as helping another at the table, can have a deep and lasting effect. I don't mean mimicking or making fun of your counterparts, but simply showing a little common humanity and warmth. This is a much preferable approach to going into a new assignment determined to 'get things done', 'shake things up', or worse, 'show who's the boss'.

4. Pleasure in learning new things

Perhaps you don't have the luxury of being a global nomad or international traveller, or of making it up as you go along like TCKs with their instinctive changing of roles. But you can learn to have 'fun' from people who have spent considerable time in more than one culture. A corporate training course doesn't always offer this. If you want to succeed as a global leader, developing the core competencies of emotional and cultural intelligence will ignite your curiosity and learning. These are essential leadership skills, and they improve with practice. The more you develop empathy as second nature, the more you will take pleasure in learning new and sometimes challenging values, approaches and perspectives.

5. Tuning into new languages, sounds and basic courtesies

I often play a little mind game. When I hear someone speaking a foreign language, however faintly it appears on my radar, I challenge myself to guess what language it is. Sometimes I am lucky and recognize words and even phrases from a language I know quite well. Other times, the guess is based on sound, appearance, and context (what is that person doing right there?). And then there are certain other clues that help, such as the movies I may have seen, the family of languages the sounds suggest, the person's expression. This is how I practice my 'getting to know you' technique. It works just as well with new or unfamiliar people. You may instinctively do the same. It's just a short step from this tuning in to learning a few words or phrases to use in a new situation or culture. Such an approach may well prove useful in the workplace with a new member of your team, or in a conference or international meeting, or on a business trip or global assignment. Tune in, learn the sounds of a few basic phrases ('hello, how are you?' 'fine, thank you') and hey, presto! You have already made a new friend and a potential long-term colleague.

6. Stepping out of the habitual and expected

When you expand into new markets or develop international teams, it's easy enough to assume that the whole world plays by your rules. However, there are countless examples of global brands making a complete hash of their expansion by remaining fixed on their *usual way of doing things*. They fail not only to research a new market but also to adapt their products to local tastes. Google mishandled its launch in China by choosing as its local brand name Chinese characters that sounded like the name of Google: *Gu* and *Ge*. Unfortunately, when translated, these characters meant 'Song of the Rice Harvest'. This slogan reminded tech-savvy Chinese consumers of their agricultural past, which effectively cut Google off from a large segment of the market. Doing what you have always done is often the mindset of Western multinationals. However, with cross-border mergers becoming ever more frequent, it's increasingly important to decentralize, embrace local brands and tastes, diversify and develop strong relationships with local leaders.

7. Nurturing and developing relationships

How do you best go about creating relationships? A good place to start is with the wider context. What do you know about the background, beliefs, tastes, customs, and values of people who may be very different to those you meet every day in your business circles? Many cultures, especially those in Asia, the Middle East and Latin America, value personal relationships above contracts, legal questions, logic, decisions, and deals. Building trust is essential in these 'high context' cultures. This trust can only come with time and through personal rapport and networks. It will not come from being overly direct. If you don't take time to develop personal relationships, you will fail. The Chinese have an expression for the foreign business types they find the most unappealing; they call them 'Track-minded Westerners'. Don't end up being regarded as a train hurtling down the track to nowhere.

8. Readiness for ambiguity, different perspectives, and contradictions

Business dislikes ambiguity. However, ambiguity is exactly what we have to deal with almost every day in the fast-moving landscape of the global economy. One of the most difficult challenges for upcoming leaders is to hold different viewpoints *at the same time*. In our Western societies we are used to facts—or we were until fake news took over the political and media agenda. Now, in addition to the 'alternative facts' generated by various political tribes, we also have to learn to accept different perspectives and even contradictions as an integral part of leadership. It's no longer easy to get a black-and-white view on a situation. The challenges of modern business are more complex. Rather than delivering a quick 'yes' or 'no' on each issue, we can learn from other cultures where 'yes' and 'no' are avoided in direct response to questions—especially when a 'no' is meant. In that way, honour and harmony are preserved. As Akio Morita, co-founder of Sony, once inscribed in a motto above the bar in his Tokyo club: 'We Japanese businessmen are amphibians. We must survive in water and on land.'

9. Asking for advice and information on appropriateness

One of the best—and least practised— ways to achieve buy-in with people of different backgrounds is to ask for advice or more information. In other words, find out what is truly appropriate. It's not only TCKs who have a mixed cultural experience. If you bow low to a Japanese person in California, as I have mistakenly done, you may offend the person bowed to because they are proud to have lived in America for decades. They expect to be considered American. Far better to find out what is usual and effective in the situation, not only in terms of respect and etiquette, but also when presenting your proposal in countries such as Japan, Singapore, Germany, and Sweden, where process is important. Everywhere is slightly different, sometimes hugely different. If your presentation is met with silence in Singapore, it doesn't mean it hasn't made an impression. It simply means it is being given serious consideration. Don't spoil it by insisting on an immediate response— find out what is appropriate.

10. Not believing my way is the only way

It is difficult to accept but sometimes you have to recognize that your way of doing things is not the only way. If you don't understand differences of approach, if you don't bother to explore these approaches, your counterparts will almost certainly resist you—or worse, ignore you. If you think, for example, that English is the business language of the world and everyone understands you, you will get a surprise. English is a second or third language for many people around the world. Local versions of Chinglish or Singlish or Frenglish make communication with regular English speakers far from clear—especially if you plough on rapidly in your mother tongue. Similarly, if you don't get support from your country or regional teams but simply roll out the plan from global headquarters, those teams will stop interacting with you. Business around the world is increasingly based on relationships and trust, which can only be nurtured through personal interactions, consensus forming, group activities, and morale building. These can take the form of dining out together, away days, participation in local festivities and customs, regular personal meetings or virtual one-to-ones via videoconferences or Skype.

4. RE-CENTERING OUR WORLDS

We seem to be in the middle of a culture war between tribalists and nativists on the one hand, and progressives and open thinkers on the other. This is also a wider clash of past and future, faith in technology and suspicion of it, and openness to immigration and suspicion of it.

This culture war will not be won by being timid or scared. The clash of beliefs will be prolonged. However, it is likely that the young will win— and in so doing they will open the way to a more enquiring, dynamic, and prosperous future.

Much will depend on the amphibians. Or rather, on those who are *amphibious*. We hear a lot about the increasing number of diverse cities around the world, and the need to protect local communities. But what's missing from this narrative is a strong thread to bind these elements together, to unify pluralistic people everywhere. Rather than attempting to ring-fence local communities, such as those in the UK left behind by globalisation, or the Rust Belt of the USA, or the estranged and fragmented regions of the European Union, we need to take a close look at what works at a local level and apply it nationally—indeed globally. We need to 'think global and act local'.

Amphibians are experienced at creating a way of life and thinking to unify the strands of their personal identity. As the world becomes more interconnected and offers greater opportunities, the example and experience of the amphibians are there to guide us.

Rather than retreat into tribes, where race conflict and fear are encouraged, we can build bridges rather than walls. Rather than seeing the world as a battleground with one group here and one group there, we can learn from the amphibians to combine viewpoints, create unexpected connections, and make something more out of our backgrounds and beliefs than the restrictions of tribal identity.

This is certainly what our younger generations are expecting from their leaders. A study conducted by the INSEAD Emerging Markets Institute and the MIT Leadership Center(6) revealed that open communication and feedback are the qualities most preferred in leaders by members of Generation X, the post-boomer generation, and Generation Y, the millennials. However, Generation Z, born from 1994 onwards, want their leaders to be more than open. They want them to be positive role models for collaboration and diversity.

Much of this difference in expectations derives from the speed of technological change. Digitalisation involves a large number of experts, but the ultimate responsibility for digital transformation belongs to all functions of the organisation. Successful change requires contribution from junior contributors all the way up to the board by linking tech-savvy millennials with the experience and wisdom of senior executives and directors.

Amphibian leaders will play an increasingly important role in bridging inter-generational gaps as well as revealing

---

6. 'Generations', a study conducted by the INSEAD, Universum, the MIT Leadership Center and the HEAD Foundation

insights that can help companies lead their workforces more effectively and compete for the next generation of global talent.

Digitisation entails disruption, which can only be navigated by exploring new business models and revenue streams. In the drive for greater agility, companies will have to launch ambitious experiments and quickly take new learning on board. This is exactly where the amphibians and next generation leaders can be role models. To build the desire and capacity to change into the fabric of the organisation, directors and senior leaders must raise their comfort levels in regard to uncertainty, ambiguity and risk. To assist in this process, amphibians are already helping boards and executives achieve unique levels of innovation, effectiveness, responsibility, and leadership.

These qualities are just as much in demand in domestic as in multinational organisations. Indeed, the workplace of many single-market companies now reflects the diversity of the societies in which they operate. Clearly, the management teams of a multinational need to be culturally diverse to operate in many different countries and to respond to global stakeholders. They must include representatives from those markets who have intimate knowledge of local customs, culture and consumer preferences in countries where the organisation operates.

However, single-market companies also need teams that reflect and leverage the multicultural backgrounds of their workforces. Since even the most homegrown of companies is now connected internationally in some aspect of their business, cross-cultural competence is fast becoming a unique competitive advantage. Cultural intelligence, which leverages personal and generational differences, reduces the possibility of conflict and encourages the pooling of ideas among team members who may not all come from exactly the same background.

The members of your teams who are amphibians will be able to handle differences more efficiently than those who have no experience of sinking or swimming. But what kind of differences are we talking about?

In the single market setting, amphibians can help with:
- Raising the morale, trust, and engagement of employees.
- Increasing talent retention and loyalty.
- Solving conflicts caused by personality clashes and opposing values.
- Creating an inclusive culture based on cultural, personal, generational, and gender diversity.
- Motivating, driving, and satisfying both customers and employees.
- Adjusting to sharp contrasts in behavioural and communication styles.
- Strengthening leaders' ability to influence customers, stakeholders, colleagues, and teams.
- Igniting leaders' inner cores so that they become the best leaders they can be.

In a multinational organisation, the amphibians can also help with:
- Reconciling multiple viewpoints about the right approach to decision-making (direct or indirect).
- Harmonising attitudes in regard to time, punctuality, and precision.

- Emphasising the creation of *trust* through personal relationships rather than logical or transactional processes.

- Exploring deference to seniority and hierarchy versus open-ended discussion and a more democratic style.

- Valuing the group rather than the individual or the individual over the group.

- Showing contrasting approaches to motivation either through processes or through incentives.

- Negotiating, networking, and communicating with global stakeholders.

- Leveraging cultural and emotional intelligence.

To convert pluralism into competitive advantage, it is not enough to simply count individual passports in a multinational organisation, concluding thereby that the management teams are diverse and representative of many countries. As the amphibians indicate, it is the mingling of viewpoints, experiences, and roles *within* yourself that counts—and these elements are not nationally or racially based. Such strands constitute a rich depository of global intelligence, which makes amphibians particularly valuable to both domestic and multinational companies.

Much depends on the length of time spent in different cultures, and above all on the readiness to absorb and learn from differences. The more curious and exploratory you are, the greater will be your resilience in complex and challenging situations.

The lives of amphibians teach us that what matters is *what you do* with your background, the viewpoints you construct by combining perspectives. If you start with this approach—thinking of every new and different person you meet as being first of all your brother or sister—then the concept of difference changes. The level of emotional connection intensifies.

True leadership is a combination of intelligence, self-awareness and emotion. In a workplace that is becoming increasingly automated—and where artificial intelligence threatens to take over some of the most basic functions—such human skill sets will become increasingly prized in the coming years.

Companies that treat people like disposable assets, and suppress emotions and intelligence, will soon run out of replacements. In the past, senior leaders have been able to make a considerable show of emotional intelligence and other caring attributes while in reality remaining closed off to their real value.

In many organisations, emotional complexity has become reduced to a binary choice between positivity and negativity ('you are either for us or against us'). And yet, as we have seen with the lives of amphibians, flexible thinking and agile emotions are a much more effective means for thriving in a changing environment.

Current or high potential leaders are best placed to handle this kind of emotional complexity if they have become amphibian: i.e. if they have built different viewpoints into their personality and background. The world of digital disruption is not simple and straightforward. It is a world where unthinking enthusiasm or blind opposition are no longer the only emotions allowed in organisations.

The intelligent global leader of the future will become an expert in reconciling different viewpoints and complex emotions.

PART TWO

*

THE TOOLS
FOR GLOBAL
LEADERSHIP

5. BECOMING BAMBOO STRONG

Diversity is the new normal and we'd better get used to it.

We are living and working in an age of rapid change: increasing globalisation and connectivity, faster time to market, more cross-border mergers and acquisitions, many new and more accessible markets, and greater mobility of workforces and teams. Even thirty years ago, we would have been able to more or less predict whom our business partners, suppliers, distributors, customers, bosses, work colleagues, and team members would be. We would have expected to interact with them safe in the certainty that most of them would be People Like Us.

Nowadays, these certainties are gone. Under the impact of migration, globalisation, and the concentration of work in super-connected cities across the world, we are dealing with people of many different national, ethnic, cultural, social, and generational backgrounds on a daily basis.

This means we are now required to develop and use a once-neglected skill—cultural intelligence—as never before. The good news is that cultural intelligence can be discovered and forged into a powerful capability for success in the new global economy. Two decades of research by scholars in dozens of countries have contributed to the evolution of the cultural intelligence (CQ)(7) Model, a simple and clear four-

---

7. CQ is the registered trademark of the Cultural Intelligence Centre, LLC, based in Michigan, Illinois.

part system for approaching culturally diverse situations and the challenges of cross-cultural encounters.

In my book *Bamboo Strong: Cultural Intelligence Secrets To Succeed In The New Global Economy* I offer a very personal exploration of the CQ Model and its four capabilities—CQ Drive, CQ Knowledge, CQ Strategy, and CQ Action—together with a methodology for creating high performing global management teams and leaders

But I also believe that, beyond the systematic application and development of the CQ Model, the real driver for success in today's globalised world is you. In other words, it's your own pliancy, adaptability, readiness to learn and to empathize. Cultural intelligence starts with the personal—with how you see yourself in different cultural situations, how much awareness you have of your own culture, personality, values and beliefs, and how they affect your thinking and behaviour.

In my own life, I've been very fortunate and privileged to travel, live, and work in many countries around the globe. I've married into families from two cultures that are very different to my own. I've had a rich variety of diverse occupations from Cambridge academic to farmer in Italy, writer in Asia Pacific, adviser to Fortune 500s to executive coach and global leadership strategist. But this does not necessarily make me unique. The fact is, many of us are now global citizens of a world where multicultural diversity exists right on our doorstep and in all aspects of our lives, from going to the gym to shopping to dining out to using social media.

I didn't start off as a global citizen. I grew up in a very different environment of People Like Us, of safe certainties, of expected behaviour and social assumptions that were typical of an Anglo-Welsh, London-born, grammar school- and university-educated boy of the time. It was only when I broke away from this background, and went to live with my first husband in Switzerland and Italy, that I discovered the elements of cultural intelligence that were to stand me in such good stead in my future life and career.

One of the central themes of this book is that you can only develop strong cultural intelligence if you are open to, and ready to learn from, cross-cultural experiences in real life. And the more of them you experience, the stronger your CQ will be.

I have made countless cultural mistakes and blunders in new cultural environments and when meeting new people from other backgrounds and countries. However, I have never allowed them to deter me from taking a risk, trying things out, stepping into the dark. The various stages of the cultural intelligence journey I guide clients and audiences through in the Bamboo Leader Workshops and Global Coaching are intended as stepping stones into this new world I discovered — a world of adventure, wonder, and celebration.

Much of the guidance I offer is personal, but in the following chapters I offer you special tools, strategies, and techniques to move you forward on your global leadership journey. For this reason, at the end of this chapter there is a link to a Cultural Intelligence (CQ) Planner on my website: **www.davidcliveprice.com/planner**.

The Cultural intelligence (CQ) Planner includes a grid of the four CQ capabilities; an assessment tool to determine your own and your colleagues' cultural profiles (see the sample at the end of this chapter); a step-by-step builder to develop your organisation's cultural intelligence strategy; and checklists and tips.

Together with the global leadership programmes laid out at the back of the book, the Bamboo Strong CQ Model is intended to provide you with all the help you need to become a confident participant in cross-cultural encounters and to build relationships, communicate, negotiate, and lead across cultures both at home and overseas—in other words, to become what I call a true Bamboo Leader.

I have taken this term, and the title of my book, *Bamboo Strong*, from the giant, woody grass that grows and transforms so rapidly when it is cut down. Bamboo easily withstands the harshness of winter. It is incredibly strong and yet flexes and bends with the force of the wind or rain. That is why the ancient Chinese regarded the bamboo as a symbol of strength, courage, and resilience.

Cultural intelligence work is often complex and challenging. It requires patience, and nuance, and subtlety, which is perhaps why more than 90 per cent of global executives identify cross-cultural effectiveness as their biggest challenge. If you have a black-and-white view of the world and of cultural issues, if you are impatient in new situations, and fearful of losing control, cultural intelligence might not be for you. However, if you can train yourself to develop your CQ, you stand a much greater chance of success in today's global economy.

This essential capability is in even greater demand in a time of mass migration, religious fundamentalism, and a ready recourse to xenophobia and political demagoguery. The world needs leaders with high CQ—not only to spread the message of tolerance but also to provide deeper and more nuanced insights into other viewpoints, conflicting opinions, and unfamiliar traditions and beliefs. It's easy to fall back on stereotype and intolerance.

The Bamboo Strong CQ Model suggests there is another way. It's a path of excitement and curiosity, of surprise and sheer delight in the discovery of other approaches and other viewpoints. I still feel thrilled when I set out in a new city, in an unfamiliar country, and I know that my cultural intelligence will guide me on my progress to new experiences and world views, to new friends and new pastures.

I hope the CQ Model laid out in the next chapter will encourage you to undertake a similar journey of transformation based on a growing ability to flex with the winds of new experiences, different ways of thinking, and unfamiliar beliefs.

Here is the first part of the assessment included in the Cultural Intelligence (CQ) Planner. To get an idea of your CQ strengths and weaknesses, answer the multiple choice questions and score yourself at the end.

CQ-DRIVE

Courage

CQ Drive is your motivation and readiness to collaborate with others in a wide spectrum of cultural settings. It focuses on your ability to gain enjoyment from and reap the benefits of cross-cultural challenges in many contexts.

Considering culture and cultural diversity in a broad sense, please answer the following questions to assess your CQ Drive.

A. If you were asked to work in another culture or country, would you

1. Pass up the opportunity if possible?

2. Find out about the expatriate life and conditions?

3. Google some information on the local culture, food and customs?

4. Ask a colleague's advice who has worked in that country?

B. When asked out to dinner by a foreign client or contact to a restaurant with 'exotic' food, do you:

1. Try a little of everything at the host's suggestion?

2. Order something very familiar from the menu?

3. Try only those dishes that look attractive?

4. Claim that your doctor will not allow you certain foods?

C. If you are going on holiday to or visiting a new country, do you:

1. Learn some basic polite phrases in the local language?

2. Get ready to speak slowly and clearly to be understood?

3. Take along a translation app on your smart device or phone?

4. Aim only to visit the 'international' areas?

D. When you are together with a person from a different culture, do you:

1. Find out a little about their background and try to connect?

2. Plan your conversation topics beforehand?

3. Just act naturally and hope it all falls into place?

4. Focus on listening to find common ground?

E. When you travel to other countries and cultures, do you:

1. Look for signs in your native language and people who speak that language?

2. Try to read some signs in a foreign language and find local people?

3. Stick to guided tours with an interpreter and guide?

4. Find your own interpreter and guide?

F. If you find yourself in a side alley in a new city with no signs, do you:

1. Look for the nearest route back to the main street?

2. Keep moving in the hope you will get to a public space?

3. Stop and look around for interesting sights and sounds?

4. Knock on the nearest door and ask for directions?

G. **If you are asked to participate in a local ritual or festival abroad, do you:**

1. Refuse saying you are new to this country and its customs?

2. Watch what the other participants are doing and imitate them?

3. Ask a local what it means and if you can participate?

4. Go with the flow and see what happens next?

H. **When finding out about a new culture, do you:**

1. Download a movie, novel, travel book or other guide to that culture?

2. Research items on the news media about that country?

3. Make friends with people from that culture in your home country?

4. See what interests, sports or hobbies you have in common with that culture?

I. **On the first evening you arrive in a foreign country, do you:**

1. Take a little walk outside the hotel or office perimeter to get acclimatized?

2. Go as far as possible into the locality searching for new experiences?

3. Get your bearings from the hotel concierge, local TV or office manager?

4. Go to bed early and face the next day refreshed?

J. In your first week in a foreign country, do you:

1. Spend as much time as possible in familiar surroundings such as the hotel pool or international restaurants?

2. Look for ways to get off the beaten track and get adopted by a local friend or family?

3. Hang out for safety's sake with people like yourself?

4. Give yourself some specific challenges to enter the local culture step by step?

INTERPRETING YOUR CQ SELF-ASSESSMENT

Circle the answer number you chose for each CQ factor and set of questions. Input your score for that answer and then add up the scores according to your answers to reach an overall total.

CQ Drive (Courage)You Scored (input your score for each set of questions below)

A.

1 = 1, 2 = 2, 3 = 3, 4 = 4

B.

1 = 4, 2 = 3, 3 = 2, 4 = 1

C.

1 = 4,2 = 2, 3 = 3,4 = 1

D.

1 = 3,2 = 2,3 =1,4 = 4

E.

1 = 1,2 = 4, 3 = 2,4 = 3

F.

1 = 1,2 = 2,3 = 4, 4 = 3

G.

1 = 1,2 = 3,3 = 4,4 = 2

H.

1 = 2,2 = 1,3 = 4,4 = 3

I.

1 = 3,2 = 4,3 = 2, 1 = 1

J.

1 = 2,2 = 4,3 =1, 4 = 3

Your CQ Drive Total Points =

OVERALL SCORES

Score: *30-40* High CQ development and leadership potential

Score: *20-30* High average CQ development and leadership potential

Score: *10-20* Average CQ development and leadership potential

Remember there is no top and bottom of the class for CQ development. All of us have the capability within us to become Bamboo Leaders with a high degree of cultural intelligence and executive maturity.

It all depends how motivated you are to draw out those intercultural skills that we have within us. Some of us have far more CQ Knowledge that we have CQ Drive; others have more developed CQ Strategy than we have CQ Action.

No one has reached perfection in any of the capabilities, far less achieved a perfect combination of all four interdependent factors. Your capacity for success lies entirely within yourself.

Once you complete the section, you are ready to take the next part of the 4-part CQ Assessment, which can be found in the Appendix and at www.davidcliveprice.com/planner

6. THE BAMBOO STRONG™ CQ MODEL

WE CAN ALL CHANGE

Did you know that the very dense fibers in each cane of bamboo give the plant extreme flexibility, allowing it to bend without snapping? In earthquakes, a bamboo forest is actually a very safe place to take shelter, and houses made of bamboo have been known to withstand 9.0-magnitude quakes. That is why, for thousands of years, bamboo has been the go-to building material for most of the world.

Some scientists believe that if bamboo were planted on a mass scale it could completely reverse the effects of global warming in less than a decade. It would also provide a renewable source of food, building material, and erosion prevention.

Trees used for conventional wood take thirty to fifty years to regenerate to their full mass. In the meantime, less oxygen is produced, less carbon dioxide is consumed, and more soil is run off in the spot where the tree is harvested— all producing harmful environmental effects. So when it comes to sustainability, bamboo has traditional lumber beaten in almost every category.

Bamboo is clocked as the fastest-growing plant on Earth. Some species have been measured to grow over 4 feet in 24 hours. A pole of bamboo can regenerate to its full mass in just six months! Bamboo can also be continuously re-harvested every three years without causing damage to the plant system and surrounding environment. Continuous harvesting of this woody grass every three to seven years actually improves the overall health of the plant. I personally witnessed the extraordinary power of the bamboo in the Tuscan valley where I lived. Every time I chopped down a bamboo cane, the same day small green shoots of a new bamboo would appear in the very same spot.

This constant regeneration made me marvel at the strength of nature.

I believe that cultural intelligence has a similar power to grow and change the world. In the thickets of stereotype, indifference, and blind hatred that we see all around us, it is the green shoots of cultural understanding, rapport, and sympathy that have the greatest chance of transforming the globe's political and spiritual ecosystem. We are living in a period of extreme migrations, of innocent refugees fleeing from political violence, of homelessness, poverty, and inequality.

People are crossing borders in flight from terrorist groups, from unemployment, and from injustice in numbers that are throwing up isolationists and protectionists as never before. Xenophobia is on the march in many countries of the world. And yet we are also living in an age of unprecedented international and multilateral cooperation. Businesses and not-for-profit organisations, educational institutions, and government agencies are collaborating in ways that are unique in history. As the process of globalisation continues, bringing with it special challenges for intercultural understanding, I believe cultural intelligence has a special power to help people change. Companies, business leaders, entrepreneurs, politicians, and academics are all engaged in this process of change and transformation.

And just like the bamboo, which grows in phases marked by stronger circles on the stem, this is a process that can only evolve one step at a time, one cultural encounter at a time, as people reach out and flex their newfound understanding. The four capabilities of cultural intelligence—CQ Drive, CQ Knowledge, CQ Strategy, and CQ Action—are not individual and isolated aspects of our attempt to make the world a better place. They are interrelated stages in the development of our cultural intelligence and of becoming true Bamboo Leaders, whether you are a current leader or a high potential leader.

So let's look at these CQ strategies, to see how they can work together to make people like you and me better citizens of this new global economy.

EXTENDING YOUR REPERTOIRE

The first thing to notice is that the different elements of cultural intelligence can be considered as stand-alone capabilities. You might, for example, be really interested in a particular culture or country (CQ Drive). And yet despite all your learning, reading books, watching movies from that country, and even learning some of the language (CQ Knowledge), you still feel completely out of it.

The only thing I remember of my first trip to Italy as a member of my high school group was being able to read the sign in Italian on the train window—È *vietato sporgersi*. I translated this to mean 'You shouldn't throw yourself out of the window' (it was actually referring to objects like tin cans). When I applied this to my thinking and behaviour around Italians, I was forever imagining that they were about to do something highly emotional—like throwing themselves out of train windows—and that I had better be on my guard.

It took me several more years, two or three more trips to Italy, and a close friendship with another Italian Renaissance scholar, Roberto, to discover a completely different and less volatile Italy than the one of my boyhood imagination (although I still thought that some Italians were too emotional for their own good).

It was only when I actually lived in Italy, not so much as a scholar researching in the *Archivio di Stato* in Modena but as a farmer with a real life in a provincial Italian town, that I took my CQ Drive and CQ Knowledge to the next level of CQ Strategy. This in turn resulted in CQ Action, such as taking part in farmers' dances, exchanging country produce, joining the olive cooperative, and writing a book about my experiences—which took me back to CQ Knowledge!

Simply having knowledge about a country or people's background is not enough to really interact with and learn from that culture. In fact, CQ Knowledge by itself might encourage a coolness and a false sense of control—like some of those British academics I knew, who studied Italian history but whose feeling for Italy was superior and distant. On the other hand, books, discussion groups, in-country planning sessions, videoconferences with global management teams and functions (CQ Strategy) can all help you prepare for the real engagement of joint projects and for CQ Action. The interaction of the four capabilities extends your repertoire of responses, behaviours, and ways to communicate with people from another background. Each capability encourages and reflects on the other, giving you much greater control over your life and work when dealing with differences—and adding to your organisation's bottom line.

THE CQ MODEL

Like the bamboo's cycle of growth, the four capabilities are in a constant state of transformation. It may be comforting to think that our CQ capabilities lead in a logical progression from CQ Drive to CQ Action and are forged together into a kind of permanent, recognizable platform like a hardware operating system. But that's not what really happens.

The four stages of global leadership development grow at a different pace and with constant variation.

Sometimes your CQ Drive lacks strength for a particular country or cross-cultural challenge. Sometimes you have far more CQ Knowledge of European markets and cultures, for example, than of Asian or Latin American markets. Sometimes you find yourself leading a multicultural team across different sectors, and you have to work hard not on your CQ Drive and Knowledge but on your CQ Strategy. At another time, CQ Action is required to implement all the information you've been storing in your head about China or Africa or the Middle East.

Just as I discovered in Italy, it could well be that your experiences in CQ Action lead you back to new reflections (CQ Knowledge) and changes in behaviour that give you much greater motivation (CQ Drive) for your next leadership challenges. The process is constantly evolving. One of your capabilities may grow more rapidly than the others. Another of your capabilities may be stuck in paralysis for several years before circumstances drive you to use it in action.

When I first arrived in Japan, I had plenty of CQ Drive to learn about this fascinating country. I also had a little CQ Knowledge gained from books, novels, movies, and a close American writer friend who had lived in Tokyo since 1950.

However, I soon discovered that my CQ Drive and CQ Knowledge were not enough to make me really enjoy living in Tokyo. I would wander around the streets looking at the Japanese and Chinese calligraphy above the shops, bars, and restaurants as if they were some kind of hieroglyphics in an alien world. I would be attracted to a certain glowing neon sign and yet would be frightened of going in there. I had no idea what would meet me inside or whether I would be immediately ejected as a *gaijin* ('outsider').

And so I continued to live in Tokyo as if I were looking at the city through a glass screen. I could see what was going on, but I couldn't participate. So I tried out some of my elementary CQ Strategy. I attempted a few words in Japanese, a phrase or two, to see if there was any response— and indeed there was. I soon became a little less of a *gaijin* in my local town and more of a respected visitor. I had a place in society. I existed.

However, this was only the first stage of my CQ Strategy. There was very little activity in the area of my CQ Action beyond the daily exchange of politeness with neighbors and shop owners. My American writer friend, Donald, was an expert on Japanese movies, life, and culture, and had lived in Tokyo since the American occupation. I therefore chose him to be my cross-cultural mentor. It was only when I allowed myself to be guided by him that I really made any progress in my CQ Strategy and CQ Action.

Donald taught me the basics of getting on with the Japanese, the little things that might make a difference in daily life in my corner of Tokyo, the way to be both polite and friendly, the things to avoid, the importance of 'appearances', and many other CQ Action tips.

So by the time I had competed a year in Japan and made my trip all around the country, I had reached a further stage of CQ Knowledge in the form of a book about my travels. I also had developed my CQ Drive, because my experience of Japanese life made me doubly motivated to succeed in Hong Kong.

There is no set process for acquiring perfect cultural intelligence or becoming a global leader or an expert in working with difference. What may have worked in one environment may well not work the same way in another culture.

What seemed the right strategy in one country may not be effective in another. We are often improvising, thinking on our feet, revising plans, and hopefully reflecting on what we are doing in our new cross-cultural encounters.

However, it is precisely because of these improvised situations, when we are suddenly called upon to react with sensitivity and understanding, that we should have a CQ model in place. The model is as useful in spontaneous situations as it is in planned assignments and projects—such as a merger and acquisition your company is undertaking.

Let's think about that merger for a moment. You work for a company based in the USA that has acquired a Singaporean business operating in several Asian countries. There are clearly a number of CQ issues that need to be addressed. Now is the time to consider your CQ model. Your leadership team could start to think of the four-part process in the following terms:

1. **CQ Drive**: Are you motivated and ready to work with your new Asia teams in culturally diverse settings? Are you able to work through the explicit or unconscious challenges and conflicts you will probably encounter?

2. **CQ Knowledge**: Do you really understand the culture and cultural differences of these new markets and how they influence behaviour? This involves knowledge of business and legal systems, family and social values, religious beliefs, as well as rules for verbal and nonverbal behaviour.

3. **CQ Strategy**: Will you be sufficiently aware of what's happening in these new cross-border encounters and able to flex by implementing CQ Knowledge and adapting to new ideas?

4. **CQ Action**: Will you be ready to focus on the appropriate verbal and physical behaviour for these diverse cross-cultural situations? Are you aware how much this will help you to build trust and respect, and minimize the chances of miscommunication?

This is just one example of the CQ model and how it could help you or your company in a similar situation. There are many other scenarios and an infinite number of solutions.

Nobody ever arrives at a perfect application of the CQ model, or indeed at a fixed point of achievement when all four elements are held in alignment. However, the leaders I have worked with in various parts of the world, and in many different sectors, have found that the CQ model is a vital tool in developing their cultural intelligence and driving up their performance and results.

YIN AND YANG

As mentioned earlier, the Chinese have a saying for the type of businessperson who comes to China intent on doing business in the rules-and law-based way that is common in Western countries. This type of businessperson is usually on a tight schedule, has definite parameters in place for the negotiations they expect to undertake, and considers the sole objective of their visit is to obtain a definitive yes or no to their proposal followed by a binding contract.

The Chinese call such businesspeople 'Track-minded Westerners'. They are fond of comparing them to a train tearing down the track that leads in only one direction.

As you can probably guess, these Track-Minded Westerners are not very popular with the Chinese. Not that the Chinese themselves are averse to results or decisions. It's just that their way of thinking is not dictated by this either/or type of Western logic that can be traced back to the Greek logician and philosopher Aristotle. They see business in more holistic, relationships-based terms. They are less concerned with either/or and more at ease with both/and. They see the various possibilities and even contradictions in a proposal that is held in tension becoming part of the relationship as a whole that gradually unfolds in the future.

This type of thinking derives from the ancient Chinese philosophy of Taoism, which is based on a belief in Yin and Yang, the opposing principles of universal harmony that are inextricably intertwined and constantly reconciled.

Much the same can be said for the principles of cultural intelligence. If you are a person who is addicted to either/or, or thinking in black and white, cultural intelligence may not be for you. Remember the image of the bamboo with its tensile strength and flexibility? Remember the amphibians? Much cultural intelligence work is based on your ability to hold two viewpoints, or maybe even several viewpoints in creative tension at the same time.

These viewpoints could be: We have to make smart informed decisions; we have to build slowly through relationships. We have to speak the basics of the Japanese language; we can get further by speaking English and playing the outsider. We have to promote our global brand; we have to adapt to local tastes and needs. We have a common humanity; we have to learn and respect cultural differences. We have to strengthen our global organisational culture; we have to leverage our local diversity.

It is obvious that in dealing with people of so many cultures and backgrounds, we are going to encounter gaps in understanding, tensions, or conflicts of various kinds. But we should see them as a cause for celebration rather than a reason for complaining. The clash and mesh of different viewpoints encourage innovation. People bring different ideas and approaches to the table, there is discussion and disagreement, and often there is a creative solution.

It is a strange paradox of our times—another cultural paradox we have to live with—that the more fundamentalist groups exert their poisonous influence in the world, the more we are ready to connect with cultures and peoples from many different backgrounds and approaches to life. To some extent this is due to the prevalence of the Internet. But it's also due to increased travel by every generation (especially the young), access to new markets, migration patterns, and simply the increasingly multicultural nature of the workplace.

Just as an educated young Chinese may now show intense curiosity about British, American, or European culture, and possibly live and work in those regions of the world, so too may a European or American person be fascinated by China and Chinese culture, and possibly live and work in China. In both instances, this curiosity will override possible skepticism about each country's political systems or 'national mission'.

This is a simplistic example but there is some truth behind it. CQ encourages complex thinking, which includes the possibility of holding two or more diverging viewpoints within us at the same time: the Yin and Yang, or the both/and principle of Taoist thought. Fundamentalism, on the other hand, insists that one way is the only right way and there is no other possible point of view.

The more the world becomes accessible, the more viewpoints we have to take into consideration and hold in creative tension. This does not mean we have to lose our identity or our authenticity. However, it is possible that sometimes we have to flex, to become almost another person, or at least to put ourselves in another's position and imagine how they are feeling.

This can do nothing but good for our mental growth and our spiritual wellbeing. When so much of the global news agenda is asking us to be this or that, to have this or that final view on pretty much everything that goes on in the world, it is salutary to have a reason to stop, reflect, compare, and feel the richness of possible diverging views. All human life is like that. It shouldn't be too much of a jump to develop our cultural intelligence and global leadership skills in the same way.

When all's said and done, people are complex. That is why the advice of intercultural books on specific countries, although often helpful, should also be observed as guidance only rather than as rigid rules of how people behave in different cultures. There are many exceptions to national traits, and we have to remember that everyone is individual, wherever they are from, and everyone is constantly developing or changing their viewpoints.

The benefit of the CQ model is that it will allow you to reflect and act on these evolving points of view, even when they conflict with your own.

STANDING BACK A MOMENT

It is not easy to find time to reflect in this increasingly frenetic era of smartphones and snap decisions, sudden disruptions in the marketplace, new modes of communication, and the daily deluge of information and emails. Standing back a moment is almost a quaint tradition of a past when people went to church and sat in pews to reflect, or trekked up mountainsides, or made a quiet excursion to a beach to watch the waves ebb and flow.

The scientifically-tested CQ Model has helped many companies, organisations and not-for-profits all around the world in a huge variety of ways. Some organisations have adopted cultural intelligence on an ad hoc basis for specific marketing and branding initiatives, global talent and team management programmes, educational and development projects, negotiation strategies, and mergers and acquisitions.

Others such as Accenture, BMW, BNP Paribas, Coca-Cola, Google, Harvard Business School, Hilton Hotels, IBM, London School of Economics, Novartis, NTT, Shangri-La Hotels, the United Nations, and many more organisations in a wide spectrum of industries across more than ninety countries have embraced cultural intelligence as an integral part of their work and as a means to raise the global effectiveness of their workforce.

I have an Australian colleague who lives in Vietnam and operates a network he calls Corporate Cultural Diplomacy, which promotes the brand and profile of companies and organisations all across Asia through staging cultural events in different Asian countries based on cultural intelligence.

CQ helps such companies build a sustainable business that captures as many customers as possible and offers them products that celebrate both the culture of the company's own country and that of the host country.

Whether adapting global business models for local markets, opening new markets, seeking a diverse customer base, leading international teams or mentoring future global leaders, developed CQ can make all the difference between success and failure.

YOU ARE NOT ALONE

I am fortunate that in my leadership work around the world I have encountered so many fascinating and highly motivated individuals and organisations. For many years, I have helped current and emerging leaders, multicultural teams, international negotiators, and other global executives accomplish their goals, drive performance, and maximize profits in a broad variety of environments.

One month I may be working with a Canadian insurance multinational aiming to adapt its leadership team to the new challenges of operating in Latin America. Another month I'm helping to establish a leadership programme in the global network of a financial institution based in London. On I may be working with the Sri Lankan government to develop programmes for its international export and foreign investment projects. Or I might be asked to deliver a Bamboo Leader Workshop for the sales and marketing teams of a San Francisco company expanding into Asia.

Together with these leaders and their teams, I work through a variety of scenarios and situations, so that their cultural intelligence becomes a natural, instinctive part of their leadership skills.

I guide them through the first phases of CQ Drive by introducing them to the CQ Assessment, so that together with their colleagues or line managers they can prepare themselves for proceeding to the next stages of the Bamboo Strong CQ Model. Once these findings are delivered and interpreted, we move on to interactive workshops and modules created for their specific challenges with CQ Knowledge and CQ Strategy, before gathering all our learning together in CQ Action plans and deliverables.

One of the most effective ways to build global leadership into an organisation is for leaders to cascade their learning down into the teams in their home office or overseas. By sharing the CQ Model with others, emerging leaders learn more about the four capabilities and develop each one further.

CQ is in essence a group-centered learning experience that is being constantly challenged and upgraded. Participants in the basic four steps of the system report a sharp increase in business innovation in their companies, which translates into increased profitability as well as a marked improvement in continuous learning and global leadership agility.

To create your own Cultural Intelligence (CQ) Planner, with action points and strategies from this chapter, please visit www.davidcliveprice.com/planner

7. GLOBAL DISC™

BRIDGING THE INTERCULTURAL/ INTERPERSONAL GAP

The second tool is the Global DISC™ Training and Certification, as accredited by the International Coaching Federation.

Globalisation has changed the world. Companies can outsource any activities: manufacturing to China, call centres to India, IT to Thailand, marketing to Facebook, distribution to Amazon. They all have access to the same opportunities. Their people are their only remaining competitive advantage.

According to a research conducted by Harvard University, 85 per cent of job success comes from having well-developed soft skills and people skills, and only 15 per cent comes from technical skills and knowledge. This makes sense. Companies can employ the best of the best from all over the world, but they are going to struggle if their people cannot work together.

Diversity is the greatest asset for a company—or liability. People often think, behave, and work in such different ways that it causes stress, confusion, and disengagement, which can lead to high staff turnover and poor customer retention.

This challenge intensifies across various cultural groups such as generations, nationalities, ethnicities, personality types, professions, and genders. Companies realize they need to motivate their people. They therefore spend a fortune on employee engagement and well-being programmes to make them feel better. However, 'spa treatments' are not going to solve the problem since they only deal with the symptoms. When their people return to work from their treatment and they cannot tolerate their colleagues, their clients irritate them and they cannot handle their boss, they become even more upset and stressed.

If you have a headache, you can take a painkiller to treat the symptom. However, that does not solve the problem if you are dehydrated or you have a more serious health issue. When people don't get along, the problem isn't incompatibility; it is usually inflexibility and lack of self-awareness—in other words, it's a lack of cultural intelligence.

It is relatively easy to fix technology by optimizing processes, but it is very challenging to work with other people. Statistically, three out of four people are significantly different to us in terms of how they think, make decisions, deal with conflicts, and express emotions. The quality of our relationships with others affects both our personal and professional life.

The top three causes of workplace conflicts are personality clashes, poor leadership, and opposing values. All three causes can be tackled by developing the capability to recognize, understand and optimize why people think and behave differently.

This does not mean simply focusing on diversity. Emphasizing diversity at the expense of inclusion has created a situation where existing members of the group feel ignored, scared, and disengaged. We can see the result of this trend in national and corporate politics. The intention might be good, but without the right skills and knowledge, diversity without inclusion turns into painful liability.

The point is not to employ the full range of skin colours, sexual orientations, and nationalities, but to create a psychologically safe and empowering environment where everybody can fulfil their potential, challenge the status quo, and drive innovation.

In cases of disagreement when different perspectives clash, the goal is to ask the right questions:

- What does the other person know I do not?

- What can the other person see I cannot?

Although this might sound obvious, in reality the answers sound rather like:

- I am right, he must be wrong. I have to prove it.

- What if she is right? I would look stupid! I cannot let it happen!

Clearly, it is easier to have people around us who are similar to us, but that is a recipe for serious conflicts and dislocations. Which is more efficient? A football team with 11 different players who have learned how to leverage their skills, or a team with 11 goalkeepers?

BELOW THE SURFACE OF DIVERSITY

According to Leadership IQ, 89 per cent of hiring failures within the first eighteen months are due to a poor cultural fit. Only 11 per cent are due to lack of skills.(8) Several other surveys reveal that 'cultural fit' plays a key role in the selection process. Companies spend a fortune on recruitment

8. Leadership IQ, 'Why New Hires Fail'

to find the right people, and then lose 75 per cent of them because they cannot get on with their managers. Employee engagement statistics reveal that middle managers receive the least amount of support from their organisations. They are stressed and employees can feel it.

71 per cent of surveyed companies say they want to have an inclusive culture, but only 12 per cent of them have managed to achieve that. According to Deloitte's research, the combination of leadership, engagement and culture is the most important and urgent of priorities. But in the same survey, the majority of CEOs revealed that although their companies tend to focus on recruiting a diverse team, they are struggling to make such teams work.(9)

Twentieth century intercultural models focus on the country of origin, on identifiable nationalities, and on our ability to notice cultural differences. However, we all belong to several cultural groups at the same time. All these groups shape our behaviour and values—and these can be rather different according to national expectations.

In fact, there are different personality types even in the smaller cultural groups as well as those with sometimes completely opposing preferences. Our personality determines how we want to behave. Culture determines how we should behave.

But in any case, how can we become an expert in hundreds of different countries, generations, professions, and personality types? Even if the country-specific national models are correct, what are the chances of meeting a statistically average person? In order to connect on an

9. 2018 Deloitte 'Culture and engagement: the naked organization', February 2015

individual level, we must learn to explore and relate to other people's background, not the other way round.

If we dig deeper, we discover that we all have the same needs and we all have our best practices to meet them. It's just that we prioritize them in a different order. On the surface, diversity looks highly complex. Below the surface, a limited number of social and psychological levers are in operation.

It is very difficult to work with people without understanding the blueprint of why they behave and think differently. Once we realise that we are all a combination of the *four personality types*—we are just conditioned differently by our environment—everything becomes simpler.

This is the basis of the Global DISC™ framework.

ACTIVE TASK-ORIENTED
Assertive and results-oriented, focused, quick decisions, likes challenges, can be aggressive and impatient, desires to lead.
DOMINANCE

ACTIVE PEOPLE-ORIENTED
Very outgoing and persuasive, people--oriented, optimistic, strong communication skills, likes to have variety in their day.
INFLUENCE

PASSIVE TASK-ORIENTED
Data, fact and analysis based. Precise and accurate. Trusts in the value of structure, standards and order. Sees the value of 'rules'.
COMPLIANCE

PASSIVE PEOPLE-ORIENTED
Very patient, favours stability and structure. Not a risk taker, likes to operate at a steady, even pace. Trust and relationships are crucial.
STEADINESS

Global DISC™ is the blueprint of why people think and behave differently depending on their personality type and cultural background, such as generation, gender, nationality, and educational level. It introduces the topic of cultural intelligence using the language of the most popular behavioural model, DISC.

It builds on what most people already know using a language they understand. It makes it much easier for them to learn about cultural differences. It also makes it easier for trainers and coaches to use as an assessment and coaching tool, as well as offering an initial and advanced certification.

The blueprint is like having the right map when we move to a new city. There is no point in using a map of New York if we have to find something in Madrid. We may push harder, we may try to think positive, but we just get lost more quickly.

Global DISC™ is a blueprint that addresses all three layers of the identity:

- **Level 1:** Your personality type, which is what a standard DISC assessment also explores by looking at what you do in various situations

- **Level 2:** Your behavioural and communication style—how you behave and communicate. This is where we have introduced five dimensions: two for communication and three for behaviour.

- **Level 3:** This the deepest layer, examining your underlying values and beliefs. This provides you with your WHY.

The Global DISC™ model provides the details for recognizing and understanding how personality traits influence behaviour. The good news is that even if people do not remember every single one of the findings, they are all distilled and seamlessly integrated into the second layer—the five DISC dimensions—to make it easier for the end user.

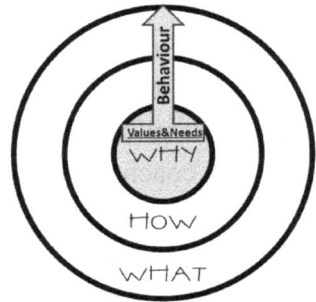

Global DISC™ helps you understand and connect with people who have different behaviour and communication styles. It distills the most researched and efficient models into one practical, internationally accredited framework designed for the challenges of the 21st century.

Focusing on both personality types and cultural background, Global DISC™ is designed for use on an individual and team level. It is not country-specific because country of origin is just a fraction of the framework. However, it is simple and efficient to use.

Many companies understand and already use DISC. It is a common language, a point of reference, which allows people to talk about sensitive and personal topics in a relatively objective way. DISC builds on the knowledge people already have and shows them how to apply that knowledge immediately.

Profitable companies do not spend money on coaching solutions simply because they have available funds. They are successful because they invest in the precise type of skills development that turns diversity into inclusion and gives their organisation competitive advantage.

Usually, companies are satisfied if they can improve their performance by a few percentage points. However, research shows that investing in the cultural intelligence of your people and leaders produces consistently good returns, with inclusion being the hallmark of the highest-performing organisations.

Diversity is the mixture of differences. Inclusion is the right mixture of people managed with cultural intelligence. One is a minefield; the other is a gold mine.

It seems clear that our success as leaders and team players is in direct proportion to our level of cultural intelligence. But rather than try to become an expert in hundreds of different countries, generations, professions, genders and personality types, we must focus on a limited number of levers beneath the surface of diversity. By revealing the structure of our personalities, Global DISC™ creates a precise process for developing intelligent global leaders of the future.

8. INTELLIGENT LEADERSHIP™ BLUEPRINT

The third and final tool in the global leadership toolkit is the Intelligent Leadership™ Executive Coaching Process and Certification, as accredited by the International Coaching Federation.

Created by John Mattone, the world's number one authority on corporate culture and leadership, and the former coach to Steve Jobs, the Intelligent Leadership (IL) Executive Coaching Process is a six- to twelve-month immersive leadership and personal growth journey that unlocks and unleashes a leaders full potential so they truly become the best, most responsive and most agile leaders and people they can be.

In a world that is increasingly driven by the forces of VUCA, digital disruption, super connectivity, migration and demographics, there is nowhere to hide.

Not even the executive suite is safe from the changes sweeping business today. In fact, the impact of those changes is felt most keenly at the executive level. CEOs, COOs, CFOs, and senior VPs—like everyone else—have to hit the ground running and keep running fast. Stockholders and stakeholders demand fast results. Teams must work more efficiently under greater pressure. High potentials and emerging leaders need to be identified and developed earlier and more effectively. Business savvy has been taken to new heights. Add to this the quest for job satisfaction and life balance, and you have the dynamic tension that creates the vital need for executive coaching.

The Intelligent Leadership Executive Coaching Process links individual effectiveness to organisational performance. It helps organisations attract and retain great leaders, enables executive teams to improve leadership and team performance, and supports senior executives responsible for making crucial business decisions and achieving outcomes. As such, it provides the 'shock absorbers' on the often bumpy road of organisational change.

The powerful advantages of the leadership development process, particularly in areas where performance goals are at risk, has moved coaching top-of-mind for executives and human resources leaders alike. Yet there is still a tremendous gap between what is expected of executives and the available resources to help them acquire both the inner-core attributes and outer-core skills and competencies required to achieve those expectations. Executive coaching aims to close that gap.

Research suggests that while executive coaching is top-of-mind for executives and human resources, only 35 per cent of organisations surveyed in executive development studies(10) utilize executive coaching as part of their high-potential development programmes. By comparison, almost half of the organisations utilize executive coaching for their VP level and above executives.

For high potentials, organisations continue to emphasize development job assignments and custom training programmes, as their primary development strategies. Two-thirds of the organisations surveyed *do not* cite executive

10. E.g. *Trends in Executive Development Research Study* (Pearson, 2011)

coaching as an important development strategy for their high potential and emerging leader talent pools.

This offers a significant opportunity for organisations, especially in light of what different generations expect from their employers (e.g. Generation X employees want a casual, independent, flexible environment, and a place to learn; Generation Y employees want a structured, supportive, and interactive environment). Above all, it is critical to understand that both generations make up almost the entirety of any organisation's future leader pool and that both generations crave continuous growth and 'connectedness' with people.

COACHING NEEDS FOR LEADERS AT DIFFERENT LIFE STAGES

It only makes sense that the thirtyish executive who has zoomed up the career ladder has different coaching needs than the fifty year old who has been in the industry since college. Often, but not always, the younger leader needs more nurturing and more directness, while the older leader is often more aware of deficiencies that need to be addressed.

Research has shown that regardless of gender, younger executives in their thirties have lower levels of self-reflection than older ones, and the changes they undergo are less dramatic than the changes of older executives. Younger executives respond to specific guidelines and concrete recommendations, but they are less likely to wonder why those guidelines and recommendations are necessary.

Executive behaviour during executive coaching also differs by age rather than generation, which is consistent with previous research describing the on-going maturation that occurs throughout adulthood. Researchers have identified three factors that they believe account for differences among younger and older recipients of executive coaching.

- Younger executives often have a self-perception of being a 'winner', and are likelier to think of coaching as a perk of being at the top.

- Younger executives have more difficulty recognizing nuances of human behaviour and are more likely to use black-and-white thinking, like "there is a single 'best' idea that should prevail."

- Younger executives are likelier to believe that there is one right way to do things, while older executives are more willing to try different approaches.

WHO USES EXECUTIVE COACHING?

Clearly, many organisations use executive coaching, because it's a $1.5 billion per year industry, with most of the biggest enterprises now using coaches. But who is it for? Executive surveys show that it is for leaders who want to:

- Improve self-confidence
- Strike a better work-life balance
- Open up new career opportunities
- Become a more effective leader

Making coaching work requires that organisations and the people running them prioritize coaching. As John Mattone says, executive coaching should never be treated as an afterthought or an 'extra', but as an essential part of developing maximum leadership potential. At the same time, it's important that companies not overuse coaching or think that coaching is capable of solving deeply entrenched organisational or personal problems. Coaching can be remarkably powerful, but it can't do the impossible.

WHAT ARE THE BENEFITS OF EXECUTIVE COACHING?

While specific outcomes of executive coaching depend on the goals that the coach and client set at the beginning of their work together, many more overarching benefits have been reported by clients and companies who have used executive coaching. Among the benefits of executive coaching are:

- Increased self-awareness
- Increased self-regulation
- Greater empathy and emotional/cultural intelligence
- Flexible thinking replacing rigid thinking
- Higher levels of motivation
- More effective leadership

Executive coaching represents a powerful strategy for meeting the continuous growth and 'connectedness' needs of future leaders.

However, there is a lot of variability in the world of executive coaching. There are effective and ineffective executive coaches. Building trust and empathy with high-potential coachees is everything and having operational experience goes a long way toward helping a coach build rapport, trust, and credibility with a coachee. It is also important to understand the 'philosophy' of the coach before considering partnering with them. They should be able to verbalize their philosophy concretely, without hesitation.

The Intelligent Leadership coaching philosophy as defined by John Mattone offers a good example:

The Intelligent Leadership process blends in-depth diagnostic assessments that identify a leader's 'inner-core' values, character, beliefs, emotional make-up and behavioural tendencies (both mature and derailer traits) with 'outer-core' assessments such as 360-Degree surveys and leadership interviews, which reveal how effectively the leader executes the 'outer-core' skills and competencies required for success.

Intelligent Leadership coaches work closely with the executive and sponsoring team to create an individual development plan that leverages the leader's enduring strengths and addresses their development needs, with a passionate focus on achieving measurable behavioural change and improvement.

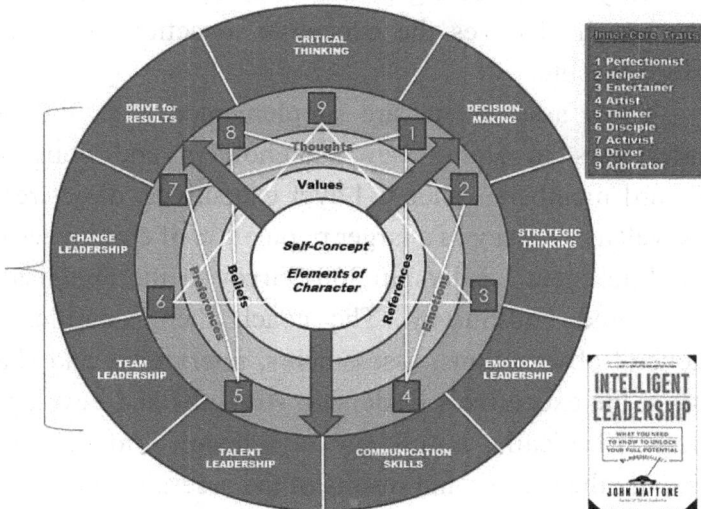

Wheel of Intelligent Leadership: "Inner-Core" & "Outer-Core"

The Intelligent Leadership Executive Coaching journey begins with a short meeting involving the executive (high potential, manager, director, vice president, senior executive, and C-level) and "sponsoring" executive/team if necessary to discuss the goals of the coaching experience, provide context and background, and discuss the proposed roadmap and coaching schedule.

The balance of the day then shifts to the executive and coach getting to know each other, both in the office and out over lunch and/or dinner. The objective over the course of the day and following day, if necessary, is for both coachee and coach to build a foundation and bond of trust and rapport.

Ultimately, the coach will assess the strength and vibrancy of both their coachee's inner-core and outer-core capabilities utilizing general observations as well as a combination of a structured in-depth interview and objective assessments, including an executive maturity assessment. One day of shadowing is almost always built in, in which the coach observes the executive in action—on calls, in meetings, etc.

These assessments are supplemented with 360-degree interviews involving key stakeholders and constituents (board members, other C-Level executives, direct reports) as well as a survey of a larger population of employees using the Intelligent Leadership 360-Survey or the organisation's sponsored 360-Survey. The coach then identifies from general observations, assessments, interviews, and shadow days, the executive's leadership strengths and development needs. Typically, a full day is scheduled to debrief and discuss the themes and results of the assessments.

The coach then transitions to introducing the executive to their Core Purpose and creating their Core Purpose

Statement (CPS). This statement captures the essence of the person and leader they want to become (and must become), what qualities they want to develop (and must develop), what they want to accomplish (and must accomplish), and what contributions they want to make (and must make). Clarity on these issues is critical because it affects everything else—the goals they set, the decisions they make, the paradigms they hold, and the ways they spend their time.

Finally, with the coach's guidance and the use of the Intelligent Leadership proprietary tools, the executive prepares an Individual Leadership Development Plan that focuses on strengthening their: (1) indisputable strengths; (2) surprise strengths; (3) indisputable development needs; and (4) surprise development needs.

JOHN MATTONE UNIVERSITY

INTELLIGENT LEADERSHIP EXECUTIVE COACHING PROCESS
4 Powerful Phases & 7 Game-Changing Pillars

The executive then meets with stakeholders and constituent groups individually and collectively to share any number of things, including their drive and passion to become the best leader they can be, and their belief that they cannot achieve this goal without input, support, and guidance from the stakeholders. The Intelligent Leadership coach provides the tools, professional development, guidance, and preparation for the executive to incorporate positive developmental suggestions from key stakeholders and constituent groups so they can finalize their Individual Leadership Development Plan.

Supported by the coach's on-going performance coaching and guidance, the current or high potential leader then begins to execute this assessment-driven plan while ensuring that key stakeholders and constituents provide quarterly feedback on the progress they are making on their leadership development journey.

It sounds like a lot but this is a process that can last from three to twelve months. During this time, the coach works confidentially with the executive on implementing powerful change strategies that leverage the coachee's leadership capabilities while also strengthening their professional development opportunities. They are first coached on strengthening their inner-core as a foundation to strengthening their outer-core leadership skills. These include cultural and emotional intelligence, and the ability to work effectively with diverse teams across multiple functions and geographies.

Overall, the strength and success of Intelligent Leadership Coaching is in direct proportion to how well the coach has created and facilitated a 'coaching process' whereby the coachee actually learns more from their stakeholder and mentor interactions than the coach. The goal of any great coach is to create a foundation of continuous self-discovery and learning for the coachee that endures well beyond the conclusion of the coaching assignment.

TYPICAL APPLICATIONS FOR INTELLIGENT LEADERSHIP

- *Competitive Advantage Consulting & Coaching*: helping executives enhance their leadership skills to stay ahead of the curve and drive business results and financial results.

- *Stretch Assignment Coaching*: creating a 'safety-net' for executives who are in critical assignments with intense time, budget, and outcome expectations.

- *High Potential Coaching:* supporting executives who are identified as leaders positioned for growth and success in the organisation.

- *Coaching for Performance*: providing focus, support and strategic business knowledge to executives whose units are behind plan and at risk of failure.

- *Leadership Development Coaching*: strengthening a leaders inner-core attributes and outer-core skills and competencies in support of organisational goals and individual leadership success.

- *Team Coaching*: helping teams rapidly assimilate new skills and behaviours.

Regardless of the application, Intelligent Leadership coaching follows a defined, consistent, multi-stage process that always promotes self-awareness, the will to change, and the execution of attributes and competencies that drive individual and organisational performance to new heights. The application of coaching, while consistent, is also customized to meet the individual needs of each coachee and the business goals of the organisation.

COACHING EXAMPLES

Competitive Advantage Consulting & Coaching

An international company has a goal of increasing market share in the USA by a certain percentage in two years. To support this goal, the senior executive team wanted to corroborate that the required competencies to meet this goal were (1) the one's they had already isolated as being critical, and (2) actually possessed by the senior leaders who were responsible for achieving this goal. The Intelligent Leadership coach implemented a Stealth Competency Mapping Process to verify that they had, in fact, isolated the critical competencies. In addition, through the use of 360 interviews, executive interviews, and the use of assessments, each leader met with Intelligent Leadership coaches to create individualized plans to improve their performance against these goals.

Stretch Assignment Coaching

An executive has been appointed the new CEO after the unexpected resignation of his predecessor following a stormy board meeting. The board has given the new CEO a challenge: turn this company around in six months. A hiring and budget freeze has been imposed by the parent company. The new CEO must get the immediate acceptance of his leadership from senior executives and quickly communicate a clear vision to the rest of the company. The previous CEO was well liked. The new CEO is reserved, but fair and objective. The new CEO enlists an Intelligent Leadership coach for help as he knows he may not get the objective feedback or advice early on that is required.

High Potential Coaching

After reviewing its succession plan, a large transportation company has identified two potential replacements for the VP of customer service role. Both executives meet with the Intelligent Leadership coach to establish goals and review the 4-step process. The coach meets with each executive's stakeholders—current VP, peers, employees, and a couple of key client accounts to collect feedback about their behavioural style, skills and competencies. In addition, each executive is assessed using the Intelligent Leadership inner-core and outer-core assessment.

The results are presented to each coachee and from there action plans are created to sustain their effective behaviours but also to improve those areas required for the new role. After months of coaching and development, each executive's stakeholders are asked to complete a Leader Watch Survey to determine if they had improved.

Results are tabulated and an additional coaching meeting is conducted to review results and set another action plan—in both cases, the executives improved in those areas identified as being critical to their success. One executive eventually was selected for this VP role; however, the other executive was selected for another VP role based on the executive's growth and development from this experience.

Developing Leadership Skills

An executive has been identified for promotion and has many of the competencies required for success, except that she is seen as introverted and shy—which will not play well in this role. Under stress, she becomes arrogant and aggressive—which also will not play well in this role. She is, nevertheless, a marketing genius and incredibly creative — assets the organisation needs in this visible role.

This leader has never been coached and has received very little feedback in her career about how she comes across. The Intelligent Leadership coach employs both 360 and objective assessments and engages in a series of coaching sessions over the next six months. This executive begins to show marked changes---she starts to open up, is more expressive and outgoing—which has a dramatic impact on her team. As she connects her new behaviour with improved results, she becomes a very strong leader and within a year has secured the promotion.

As the above examples show, Intelligent Leadership™ offers highly focused and responsive solutions for specific coaching challenges within organisations and global leadership teams.

Together with Bamboo Strong™ Global Coaching and Global DISC™, Intelligent Leadership provides an empowering and inspiring guide for current and emerging leaders, global companies and executive coaches to thrive in the new digital economy.

PART THREE

*

THE HIGHWAY TO GLOBAL LEADERSHIP

9. ONLY CONNECT

We are all on a cultural intelligence journey every day of our lives in this rich, complex, and sometimes deeply unsettling world. In our businesses, families, and relationships, we connect as a matter of course with people from every culture. I am by no means different in talking regularly via Skype to clients and contacts in Australia, Brazil, the US, France, Japan, and Hong Kong, to name just a few of the countries and locations. Whether for business, family, or pleasure, I get on a plane to Denmark, Singapore, Italy, South Korea, or even Myanmar as if it were nothing special, as if the destination were just around the corner.

In this sense, I am something of a mini-multinational, just like millions of entrepreneurs and small- or medium-sized businesses like me around the world—and millions of tourists too. Through my life experiences, I am an amphibian. Even at home in London, I interact regularly with different members of multicultural teams in companies both large and small, as well as with their corresponding teams in countries all over the globe. Almost everything I do involves some kind of cross-cultural element. I exercise three times a week at my local gym by the River Thames in a BodyPump class where it only recently occurred to me to count how many nationalities were in the studio.

The result astounded me. I discovered that I take regular exercise with BodyPumpers of around thirty-five nations, of which just two 'locally grown' fitness fanatics (including myself) represent the UK. Our instructors are Brazilian, Cypriot, Hong Kong Chinese, and Latvian. And yet, until I did my little study—which eased the pain of the countless lower-half lunges—it did not occur to me that there was anything special in our thrice-weekly cultural mash-up. Or rather, it occurred to me on some level where my cultural intelligence was on automatic—the space where I translated what was said to me in different versions of English, with a few Portuguese or Greek words thrown in, and where I instinctively modulated my own Cambridge English to chime with different ways of speaking the language.

In other words, my BodyPump class is a microcosm of what I have trained my cultural intelligence to do over the past forty years: tune in, accept, interpret, respond with similar intonation and even choice of words, harmonize, gain trust, stand in others' shoes, make friendships, gain benefits.

I don't know whether this strikes a chord with you or not. It's only a simple example, but I'm sure if you think over your daily routine in your workplace or at home you might come up with similar examples of almost unnoticed adapting or, as some of the cultural intelligence studies call it, 'flexing'. It may be the way you talk with your local corner shop owner on the way to work, or the regulars at your coffee shop, or colleagues on your team, or your boss. It's something we do in the face of the incredible diversity of our world, both in the workplace and when communicating via virtual networks. We try to get on the other person's wavelength.

We may not be very good at it. We may have little experience of it. We may be better with understanding and adapting to some cultures rather than others. But I think, if you go deep inside, you will catch glimpses of moments when this reaching out or flexing, or whatever you want to call it, really worked for you. A moment of much deeper understanding. A moment of curiosity crowned with a flash of enlightenment. A moment of greater tolerance, or compassion, or simply human warmth. A moment when you bridged that gap with a person from another background almost without thinking—and yet retained the essential being that is you, with all your values and beliefs intact.

A person who regularly achieves this level of understanding and flexibility has the potential to become an intelligent global leader—or as I call it, a Bamboo Leader. The bamboo bends in the wind, but it is inherently very strong. It is still used for scaffolding in some parts of the world. It flexes with wind and rain, and even snow, but always springs back. It has an empty center with space to be filled.

In other words, the bamboo presents both empathy and strength. As the world becomes more multipolar, more connected, and more multicultural, we need to develop the qualities of the Bamboo Leader in ourselves.

We are living in a period of extreme migrations, of innocent refugees fleeing from political violence, of homelessness, and poverty, and inequality. People are crossing borders in flight from terrorist groups, from unemployment, and from injustice in numbers that are throwing up isolationists and protectionists as never before. Xenophobia is on the march in many countries of the world.

And yet we are also living in an age of unprecedented international and multilateral cooperation. Businesses and not-for-profit organisations, educational institutions, and government agencies are collaborating in ways that are unique in history. As the process of globalisation continues, bringing with it special challenges for intercultural understanding, I believe cultural intelligence has a special power to help people change. Companies, business leaders, entrepreneurs, politicians, and academics are all engaged in this process of change and transformation.

And just like the bamboo, which grows in phases marked by stronger circles on the stem, this is a process that can only evolve one step at a time, one encounter at a time, as people reach out and flex their newfound understanding.

Of course when I talk about a 'cultural intelligence journey', I don't mean that we are all more or less passengers bound in the same direction as soon as we consciously step on our Cultural Intelligence Express—and that we're all going to end up at the same destination once we have crossed similar mountains, and rivers, and national borders, and cultural barriers.

We all respond differently to the challenges of this complex, cross-cultural world of ours, and each one of us is different and individual. We will have personal and individual reactions to different cultural settings and scenarios. It is by no means certain where we will end up, even when we have developed our cultural intelligence over many years and in many different situations.

For some people—and these tend to be the majority—it is extremely difficult to function successfully when confronted with cultures, personalities, and attitudes that are not very similar to their own. Even when they are posted to other countries in their jobs, they often fail to adapt to the prevailing culture or to even set foot outside their own safe expatriate ghetto. They want everyone they encounter to be 'just like me' and to do things 'just like at home'. And when that doesn't work out for them, they complain to their expatriate colleagues that they don't 'get' the Chinese, or the Brazilians, or the Indians, or even the colleagues themselves.

They want a system that will enable them to interact safely with the locals, or people in a new team, without having to make any adjustments in their values or behaviour. Lists of dos and don'ts are often the main support that such professionals use (if they use any), as if a quick rundown of etiquette tips will save them the painful business of overcoming personal differences and communicating effectively.

This shopping list approach to cultural adjustment is perhaps better than making no effort at all. However, it is unlikely to work when you are confronted (as we all are, sometimes several times a day) by a multiplicity of different cultural situations—personal, generational, or organisational. How do you handle the East Asia portfolio of clients you have been handed when you are told the Japanese are different to the South Koreans, who are different to the Mainland Chinese, who are different to the Taiwanese? How do you avoid stereotypes when you rely on your etiquette tips and shopping lists? How do you treat a Japanese American differently to a Tokyo-born Japanese?

Don't get me wrong. A list is an attempt at understanding or fitting in, but it won't help you respond effectively to a variety of cultural contexts. You will become confused when trying to remember what to do when and in what culture. You will get cultural overload, and you will do what many stressed people do: say it's all a waste of time, stick to your guns, and not bother.

This is a great shame because with a little help to flex your cultural muscles, you could end up like I have in my

BodyPump class. You could instinctively adjust to different peoples from different cultures almost without noticing you are doing it. After the class is over, I spend some time exchanging a few words in Italian with Fabrizio, the barista at the club's coffee bar. Fabrizio clearly enjoys these little chats and often offers me a salmon and salad panino on the house to accompany my double macchiato. It is not a premeditated ruse on my part. I don't have a list to tell me that Italians like hand gestures and exaggerated flattery. I just do what comes naturally. I try a little cultural intelligence and *voilà!* (Or rather, *ecco!*)

You might say that all this proves is that we should treat people as individuals. And you would be right. Beyond the cultural differences, we often find that people are the same all over the world. As we have discussed in earlier chapters, they have the same needs, and insecurities, and loves, and dreams that we have.

However, to discover and celebrate this, you have to make some effort to get on the same wavelength, to reach out and communicate, and above all, to respect others' beliefs and traditions. Cultural intelligence, which also includes cultural sensitivity, helps you to do this.

When I lived in Switzerland, I discovered that speaking English did not make me a trusted member of the Swiss family into which I had married, not even High German did. I had to speak Swiss German and *make the effort* to become accepted. If you take the example of Switzerland out into today's global economy, you will find that English being spoken almost everywhere does not mean that we are all more less the same and on the same wavelength. There are many local versions of English, all with their own dialect and expressions and meanings. English is also a second or perhaps a third language in vast areas of the planet. Your English is not necessarily my English. You are not me.

Yes, we are living in an era of extraordinary innovation, convergence, and connectivity. However, the great paradox is that the more we are connected, and the smaller the world seems, the more we have to respond effectively to new markets and cultures that were previously hidden from us. We are virtually present now and sometimes physically present in Shanghai and Bangalore, in Yangon, and Sao Paolo. How do we grasp the opportunities? How do we communicate? How do we show the necessary respect and not come over as Neanderthals with an excess of arrogance?

If you want to succeed as a Bamboo Leader, you will have to speak the equivalent of some Swiss German in a world of English. You will have to relate, to listen, to adapt, and only then will you develop the skills to be an intelligent global leader.

10. BEYOND DIVERSITY

Acquiring cultural skills is a significant challenge for leaders and teams in a global environment. However, it is equally important for leaders to focus on the personal strengths and shared values of team members whatever their nationality or cultural background may be.

A team comprised of possibly five or six nationalities will not necessarily succeed if national characteristics and differences are the only area to be addressed. A trustful environment based on personal strengths and behaviours is much more likely to foster collaboration than a strategy that solely emphasizes cultural differences.

People of many backgrounds and influences, including mixed race, are to be found in all countries —particularly among the millennials and Generation X. Their common experiences in an interconnected world, especially travelling and working in matrix teams, make them far less susceptible to 'culture shock' and more open to finding common areas of approach, values, and behaviour.

Rather than encountering a 'Brazilian' or 'Chinese' team, new leaders and team players need to explore and harness the rich variety of similar experiences, personalities, ideas, and visions they share with each other. These will have greater influence on their behaviour and achieve better results than a dos and don'ts list of cultural etiquette.

The aim is not to create another tribe by studying hundreds of different cultures (there's always more than one, and often several within the same person). It is rather to accept the fact of diversity, leaving the more obscure and sensitive subject of cultural adjustments until later to find expression naturally.

CULTURE SHOCK – OR NOT

Celebrating diversity by understanding cultural differences and showing how diverse your organisation is will not necessarily create a successful organisation or outstanding leaders. Rather than simply counting the number of initiatives centering around gender, skin colour, sexual orientation, religious beliefs, or ethnic background, organisations should aim above all to create an inclusive work culture.

When the emphasis is on *inclusion* rather than diversity, the underlying drivers of excellent team performance and leadership foster a culture of creativity and innovation. Ideas are shared and strengthened, not because of diversity but because of inclusion.

Any emerging or high potential leader may struggle for a while in a new environment. Some continue to struggle despite (or because of) their previous track record in previous locations or assignments. Their whole network, knowledge, and confidence need to be rebuilt in the new environment.

That's when people talk about 'culture shock'. However, those who don't succeed in a new posting often continue to blame culture shock for their failure—with a remarkable 67 per cent of expatriates failing repeatedly in new overseas or international team assignments.(11)

11. Deloitte, 'Culture and Engagement; the naked organization' (2015)

Culture shock is not necessarily to blame. The question is not how to handle cultural challenges but whether the leader can bring to the new team some of the leadership attributes and inner-core qualities that worked well in interactions with previous teams.

Those who do succeed in new assignments and postings seem to have an innate mental flexibility and inclination to enjoy the shared 'cognitive diversity' of their new teams or client base. They have an inner resilience and strength, which enables them to thrive in every new situation.

These leaders use cultural shortcuts rather than learned cultural agility to succeed. For example, they adopt a bare lexicon of 2-3 basic greetings and 2-3 basic taboos to guide them through in new environments. They simply use this mental shorthand to sidestep any cultural barriers and move forwards.

I recommend this method in Chapter Three, particularly in the early stages of adjusting to a new environment. Indeed, I have practiced it myself in many countries around the world. If you reach out in South Korea with *Annyogi kaseyo* for 'hello' and *kamsa hamnida* for 'thank you very much', you can forge a new relationship very quickly.

Successful leaders seek out the psychological drivers of their new team members, colleagues, or clients: personality, profession, age, gender, etc. In the Global DISC™ assessment discussed in Chapter Seven, drivers such as dominance and influence are identified, with the results built into a data-rich report on the participant's personal, generational, and cultural profile.

The inner and out core assessments of the Intelligent Leadership™ Process also measure a leader's predominant traits and relative maturity ratios. Using such granular data, as well as 360 assessments and stakeholder feedback, the leaders discover their two *indisputable strengths* and their two *surprise weaknesses*. They then incorporate these findings into an initial leadership development plan—with particular reference to a specific work assignment, project, or challenge.

This evidence-based behavioural approach raises team performance, especially in new or challenging situations. By analyzing the results, leaders discover who has the more dominant style in their teams, who may be a powerful activist with derailer traits such as bullying, who is a natural arbitrator with potential weaknesses such as merging into the background, or letting things go. This inner psychological map will guide them far more accurately—and far quicker—than simply studying cultural differences in new situations.

CREATING A COMMUNITY

In its broadest sense, culture intelligence enables leaders to leverage personal *and* cultural differences. That means respecting the individual diversity of profiles and character.

The goal is not to create another silo or closed off tribe, but an open community in which diversity of viewpoints and personalities, rather than cultures, prevail. If you let cultural attitudes guide you alone, you may well end up as a marketing director I coached discovered when working with a new sales team in Singapore and Malaysia.

Because she thought that Asians respected seniority, she let them know early on 'who called the shots'. She was then surprised that the team met her every move with silence. Puzzled by their non-cooperation, she decided that reticence was a Southeast Asian characteristic and tried cajoling them into action.

Finally, she wrote to each one of them individually asking what their challenges and concerns may be, and promising to address them. Both the Singaporean and Malaysian teams responded with strong, appreciative voices and positive suggestions for creating the way forward. They simply expected to be included in the consultative and decision-making process.

CASE: CUSTOMER SATISFACTION AND EMPLOYEE ENGAGEMENT IN THE LUXURY HOTEL INDUSTRY

The UK tourism sector is large and growing. Output has increased by over 5 per cent per year for the last decade, and will increase by a similar amount over the coming decade. Some of the most current trends and insights:

- Customers are becoming more demanding, driving up the level of service expected. Managers and staff need to develop a culture of continuous improvement to meet these increasing expectations.

- The sector needs to improve productivity and attract and retain talent. Poor perception of parts of the sector (low pay and unsociable hours) can make it difficult to attract staff. Tourism has the highest labor turnover rate of any sector.

- Not enough investment in the workforce. The sector has a relatively high level of spend per employee on training, but much of this is the cost of training new recruits as a result of high labor turnover.

- Employers need to invest in staff and increase employee engagement. A more motivated workforce will lead to improved customer satisfaction, increased revenue and profits, and reduced staff turnover.

- 21 per cent of employers report skills gaps and many say that their staff does not have the necessary customer service and management and leadership skills they need.

CURRENT ENVIRONMENT

- Employee engagement is critical in helping businesses maximize the potential of their staff, and excel at customer service. Three quarters of businesses feel their employees are quite engaged or very engaged at work. However, some businesses do nothing to engage their staff, as they don't believe their employees intend to stay in the job.

- Productivity is lower in service sectors than other sectors of the economy, and also varies more across the sector. Labor productivity performance is highly linked to demand, as employers need to retain core staff even when demand falls. This requires effective and efficient management.

- Customer expectations are driving up the level of service expected.

CUSTOMER CHALLENGES

The client is one of the UK leaders in the luxury hotel business space providing the ideal location, for business and leisure, in beautiful surroundings across over 30 venues throughout the UK with a portfolio of flexible properties – from contemporary London business centres to listed country houses.

> **Challenge 1** – Established management and leadership styles and practices were causing high staff turnover, decreased employee engagement and personal conflicts.

> **Challenge 2** – Hotel guests were increasingly drawn from a diverse global clientele with high expectations based on their own cultural background and preferences, which often ran counter to the current, rigid customer service style.

PRELIMINARY ASSESSMENT

Jon Maxwell said that 'leaders become great not because of their power, but because of their ability to empower others'. This principle is important to the hotel chain; so too is specific knowledge to understand what motivates and drives employees from three generations and eight countries with different personality types.

As a standard, the company had a dominant leadership and management style, which was applied to all members of staff independently of the circumstances. The same procedure was visible in the style of the five-star level customer service, which followed strict rules with little space to customize the product according to the situation or customer.

Six weeks prior to the training, the Global DISC™ assessment was conducted along with a series of interviews. The results showed that 80 per cent of the conflicts, complaints and lack of engagement within the workforce was due to personal differences in communication and behaviour between managers, employees, and customers. Only 20 per cent was attributable to technical faults, wrong forecasting, and accidents.

PROPOSED SOLUTION

In order to address these findings, a comprehensive training programme was developed in conjunction with the organisation's executive team. The objective of the training was to develop the necessary global leadership, communication, and conflict resolution skills required by employees to meet the needs of the hotel chain's upscale and diverse customer base.

A pilot programme was rolled out in the 150-year-old, iconic flagship hotel of the chain. The building has 200 bedrooms, 11 meeting rooms, 2 restaurants and 1 spa.

Training based on the Global DISC™ principles and results was rolled out to 26 of the hotel employees. The duration of the training was one full day. Two weeks later, a refresher session was held, followed by ongoing, on-the-job coaching by managers and peers.

Over this period, the hotel chain transformed its personal and cultural diversity into an inclusive environment where engaged employees provide outstanding customer service regardless of the clients' nationality, language, political, or religious background.

11. THE FUTURE IS HERE AND NOW

As we have seen, today's new generation of business leaders require increasing resilience and flexibility to navigate and respond to the challenges of a rapidly changing and volatile world. They have to cooperate and communicate well with diverse teams and act on instructions that are complex, multidimensional and often international. They have to handle fast-evolving relationships at all levels, and often in many departments and regions, without becoming stressed, disengaged or confused. And they also have to respond to the evolving needs and expectations of their diverse clients.

To meet these challenges, leaders must develop their cultural and emotional intelligence as never before to achieve their full potential, enhance productivity and deliver the very best solutions.

To show the process in action, here are some more examples from the Bamboo Leader toolkit.

CASE: TARGETED LEADERSHIP DEVELOPMENT PLAN RESULTS IN DOUBLE DIGIT GROWTH IN SIX MARKETS

Industry: Retail

Client: Beauty products; 6 markets in Asia Pacific, China, and Europe

Scenario: The client is aiming to expand its core business model building on long-term success and sustainable profits in Hong Kong and Macau. However, although it initially gained market share in Malaysia, Singapore, Taiwan and UK, it relied too much on simply replicating the Hong Kong business model and products globally. In addition, it failed to focus on a leadership pipeline based in its new markets, and hoped that sending people from its core market to manage and recruit middle management locally would suffice. The result was misalignment and lack of leadership in unfamiliar markets, especially in China.

Approach: A customized high performance leadership development programme was created and facilitated, with a two-way interchange of new and experienced leaders between the company's core market and its expanding markets. A series of two-day Bamboo Leader Workshops (see below) was held to focus on leadership capacity, strategy and execution. By working individually with senior leaders in Hong Kong, Malaysia and China, a 'core cadre' of senior managers was built across geographies and functions who could in turn transfer their skills and knowledge to the leadership teams in other markets.

Results:
- The client is now ranked #2 overall in market share in Asia Pacific.
- The client increased revenues by 10%+ YOY (4 consecutive years).
- The China business began to break even after several years of losses, using local leaders for each 'region' coached in Hong Kong and Malaysia.

- Empowered managers are responding more effectively to rapid changes in the online market, consumer preferences and buying habits.

- Trust is growing among different teams, businesses, departments and regions.

- The new logistics management solutions helped reduce costs by up to 25%.

CASE: 30 PER CENT RISE IN MERGER'S PRODUCTIVITY FROM STRATEGY AND LEADERSHIP PLAN

Merger of Group's UK and UK operations with an Asia Pacific insurance company.

Industry: Insurance Services

Client: Multinational, US, Europe, Asia

Scenario: Following the merger of the Group's operations with a leading Asia Pacific insurance company, the Strategic Leadership Team in the US and UK struggled to align themselves with the Hong Kong and Singapore teams. They knew there were differences of business approach and mindset but did not know how to solve these with occasional 'parachute' business trips and videoconferences. Communication was poor between geographies, and business processes were hampered by what the Western team perceived as an overly hierarchical and conservative approach to decisions in the Asia Pacific teams.

Approach: A strategic learning and leadership development plan was created and facilitated for the Strategic Leadership Team in all geographies. The Bamboo Strong CQ Assessment was administered to individual members of the global leadership teams. Through a series of twice monthly group Masterminds, further assessments and one-to-one Executive Coaching, both sets of teams were then guided to work together on overall issues such as collaboration, decision-making and teamwork, as well as on their approaches to specific business challenges in different jurisdictions.

Results:

- A clear action plan was developed to ensure alignment and buy-in of management across the organisation.

- Foundational knowledge and background/culture of various jurisdictions in which the company did business were strengthened.

- A shared approach was created for business meetings, decision making, referrals and meet and greets.

- Efficiency and productivity rose 30% over two years.

- Lagging parts of the business became profitable in less than 18 months

- All SLTs estimated their workload had decreased by more than 40% within the two-year window.

BAMBOO LEADER WORKSHOP AND RETREAT

This personalized, intensive and transformational Bamboo Leader Workshop can be tailored to specific needs and markets and comes in various formats from bite-sized (1.5 to 2 hours) to Weekend Retreats.

The programme is designed for CEOs, senior executives, and high potential leaders to dramatically increase their global leadership and team management skills while it also addresses challenges that pre-globalisation solutions are unable to resolve.

The programme includes the Global DISC™ and Cultural Intelligence (CQ) assessments, the book *Bamboo Strong: Cultural Intelligence Secrets to Succeed in the New Global Economy* with foreword by Dr Marshall Goldsmith, two rounds of one-to-one debriefings and individual coaching, interactive workshop(s), follow-ups, and results measurement for ROI.

Step 1: Cultural Intelligence (CQ) Assessment
- Take the CQ psychometric assessment to assess your current cross-cultural and leadership effectiveness and awareness.

- Identify the key cultural differences that may affect or influence your relationships at work with your customers, business partners, colleagues, and staff.

Step 2: Building Cultural Awareness – CQ Drive
- Develop your motivation, courage and readiness to collaborate with others in a wide spectrum of cultural settings.

- Enhance your ability to reap the benefits of cross-cultural challenges in many contexts, markets, and workplaces.

Step 3: Creating Cultural Competency – CQ Knowledge

- Leverage knowledge of differences in business and legal systems, family and social values, religious beliefs, and rules for verbal and nonverbal behaviour to maximize profits.

- Enter others' mindsets so you can build a culturally sensitive team that enhances productivity and performance.

Step 4: Sharpening Leadership Skills – CQ Strategy

- Develop a 360 perspective for exactly what's happening in a cross-cultural encounter and then strategize accordingly.

- Plan effectively on the basis of that understanding to implement new knowledge and ideas.

Step 5: Achieving Transformation – CQ Action

- Enhance your ability to 'flex' mentally, to avoid miscommunication and create trust based on your newfound confidence.

- Leverage your leadership agility to build relationships, network, negotiate and manage across diverse cultures, backgrounds and borders, in new markets and in the multicultural workplace.

What Results Can You Expect?

The Bamboo Leader programme enables delegates to become flexible, responsive leaders without being experts in hundreds of different cultures and backgrounds. This powerful combination of validated assessments, best-selling content from across the globe, and personal guidance helps participants:

- Adapt their leadership and management style to other people in the workplace, at other levels in the organisation, or in international teams.

- Improve their communication, confidence and trust with managers and colleagues in other regions or countries.

- Understand and leverage personal, generational and cultural differences in working relationships.

- Adapt to different approaches to business in new client situations and overseas jurisdictions and avoid giving offence.

- Develop solutions within existing programmes to upgrade them to the 21st century, post-globalised world.

Bamboo Leadership is *not* simply based on common sense and good intentions—there are proven, simple and efficient frameworks that enable excellent local leaders to become outstanding global leaders who in turn impress and influence clients and colleagues regardless of their background. It all depends on YOU!

To create your own Cultural Intelligence (CQ) Planner, with action points and strategies from this chapter, please visit Appendix or www.davidcliveprice.com/planner

POSTSCRIPT: YOUR FUTURE GOALS

BAMBOO GLOBAL LEADERSHIP

I have tried to give you the insights, the strategies, and above all the personal motivation to develop the mindset of an intelligent global leader. As the Age of Pluralism gathers pace, and our backgrounds become increasingly heterogeneous and intermingled, we need leaders who can manage change and diversity by leveraging both personal and cultural differences. In the face of such intense VUCA pressures, the leaders who succeed will be flexible, resilient, and responsive in many new and changing environments—whether these are in their functions and geographies, in their virtual teams, in new or unfamiliar markets, or as a result of digital disruption and increased connectivity.

Standing in other people's shoes has never been more important as a capability for global leaders. It sounds simple, even banal. But it is a core necessity of our challenging times. We have to hold different viewpoints in our minds, sometimes at the same time in a kind of creative tension. We have to embrace complexity and see things from different angles. Bamboo Leaders embrace vulnerability within themselves as one of their core strengths. They are not all seeing and all knowing. They understand that the black-and-white view is a failure to genuinely think, and that accepting their weaknesses as well as strengths is the path to greater leadership.

So when it comes to rallying a global team or holding an international videoconference, or arranging a face-to-face meeting with team members travelling to an agreed venue, the Bamboo Leader will make sure that the meeting leadership rotates among attending groups and countries. They will pay attention to such 'minor' differences as the time zones and when it is morning or evening for the attendees (or even the middle of the night!). They will consider national holidays and festivities.

They will also make allowances for different levels of spoken English or the common language, such as French or Spanish or Chinese, that is bring spoken. In these and countless other ways, the leader will work hard to *include the diversity and viewpoints of the attendees*, as well as rotating the agenda to focus on the concerns and challenges of each geographic team.

So much of global leadership and collaboration is to do with being valued. This is particularly true for high potential and emerging leaders. These younger leaders need above all to feel *connected*, and for many of them connection also means being mentored. As we saw in the Global Leadership Forecast(12), only 14 per cent of a thousand C-Level executives worldwide believe they have the leadership talent to execute their upcoming strategy. An extraordinary 64 per cent identified the development of Next Generation leaders as one of their Top Ten challenges (implying the challenge has not been met).

This shortfall represents a major opportunity for internal coaches and mentors, as well as business and executive coaches. As more and more established leaders retire from

12. 2018. Published by Development Dimensions International and the Conference Board

their organisations, Generation X and Y leaders will have to fill the gap. But are they equipped to execute their new roles? It seems not. Indeed some 52 per cent in the survey believed that they are not at all equipped.

This book is intended not only for current and emerging leaders, but also for their executive and internal coaches. The key to Bamboo Leadership is great coaching, both externally and internally. That is why I have included three essential tools to coach global leaders, and to certify the coaches themselves in these programmes (see also Appendix):

- Bamboo Strong™ CQ Assessment and Global Coaching
- Global DISC™ Training and Certification
- John Mattone's Intelligent Leadership™ Executive Coaching and Certification

Each of these coaching models by themselves will strengthen the leadership pipeline. However, when used as complementary frameworks they form an irresistible and compelling solution to develop Bamboo Leaders of the future, as well as outstanding executive and business coaches.

Huge multinationals like Google and Walmart have lost billions of dollars in China or other global markets because they have simply not invested in their global leadership and competencies. Almost every week comes a new story of a failed or ailing international merger because of a lack of alignment, inflexible 'headquarter blindness', and the inability of teams to work together—not due to culture shock but because of personal incompatibility and poor engagement.

As the peoples of the world become increasingly plural, reflecting a huge range of influences from education, to travel, to social media, to generational preferences, intelligent global leadership is not an optional 'extra' for 21st century organisations. It is an urgent necessity.

Due to the opening up of so many markets, the super-connectivity we experience daily, and the changing balance in the global economic system, we have a unique opportunity to reach out, be curious, learn, adapt, and richly benefit from a position of strength—not of weakness. That is what it means to be a Bamboo Leader.

Although this is the end of this book, that doesn't mean it has to be the end of our work together. In the preceding chapters, I have given you a series of insights and action steps such as the Bamboo Strong CQ Assessment to guide you to greater leadership, personal fulfillment and abundance. Are you ready to complete the assessment in the Appendix and create an Action Plan? Your success directly corresponds to the steps you take.

If you need more help, part of your Action Plan could be a Bamboo Leader Workshop or Seminar as laid out in the previous pages. I can help you or your organisation with your executive coaching and intercultural training, and I can also assist you to become a certified coach in the Global DISC and Intelligent Leadership programmes. An outline of both courses, which are International Coaching Federation (ICF) accredited, is included in the Appendix.

Finally, to work directly with me or to obtain advice and support about all the strategies I've discussed in this book, you can visit www.davidcliveprice.com or email me at david@davidcliveprice.com.

I am thrilled that you have taken time out of your schedule to read my book and listen to my guidance. Developing your global leadership will make your world more alive, more comprehensible, and more inspiring. I want to continue to serve you and help you to achieve all your dreams, hopes, and goals. I also would like you to share with me your stories of achievement and let you read about others at my website and in my books. In whichever way we share, I very much look forward to helping you on your journey to becoming an outstanding Bamboo Leader.

And if there is anything I can do to be of service, please just ask.

David Clive Price
www.davidcliveprice.com
info@davidcliveprice.com

HOW TO REACH DAVID CLIVE PRICE

Participate in a Bamboo Leader Training Course, Workshop, or Mentoring Programme

These are vibrant, kick-start, inspirational events and courses that will challenge your normal patterns of thinking and feeling and provide you with a comprehensive system to enrich your business and your life.

Learn more at http://www.davidcliveprice.com

Bamboo Strong programmes:

http://www.davidcliveprice.com/coaching

The *Bamboo Strong* book:

http://www.davidcliveprice.com/coaching

Asia coaching programmes:

http://www.davidcliveprice.com/asia-coaching

The Master Key to Asia book also by David Clive Price:

http://www.davidcliveprice.com/master-key-asia

The Master Key to China book also by David Clive Price:

http://www.davidcliveprice.com/master-key-china

SPEAKING

To discuss David's availability for speaking at your live event or for interviews on telesummits, podcasts, in print or on live media, please email us with your requirements to info@davidcliveprice.com

David speaks:
http://www.davidcliveprice.com/global-leadership-speaker
David's keynote topics:
http://davidcliveprice.com/leadership-topics
Testimonials to David's speaking:
http://davidcliveprice.com/testimonials

Follow David on Twitter: **@davidcliveprice**
Join David on LinkedIn: **https://uk.linkedin.com/in/davidcliveprice**

BECOME A BAMBOO LEADER

Thousands of executives, business owners, and professionals have achieved success thanks to the advice and systems in this book. You can too.

ABOUT THE AUTHOR

David Clive Price, Ph.D.
International Bestselling Author and Speaker

As a global executive coach, David is passionate about leadership and management development, talent and engagement and brings more than thirty years of experience of senior leadership coaching, strategic advisory and change management roles to his delivery of global leadership programmes.

Building on his own learning as chief Asia speechwriter and cultural integration specialist for HSBC, David has coached and advised leadership teams for many global organisations, including AIA, Standard Chartered, Credit Suisse, Santander, Julius Baer, and Morgan Stanley, as well as political and trade leaders.

Speaking English, French, German, Italian, and Cantonese, and having lived and worked in numerous countries, David's multicultural experience informs all his executive coaching, as well as his bestselling book *Bamboo Strong,* with foreword by Dr Marshall Goldsmith.

He is a visiting lecturer on global leadership at the University of Greenwich Business School, holds a PhD in Renaissance History from Cambridge University, and often appears in the media, including BBC Radio, The *Wall Street Journal, Business Insider,* and *International Business Times.* His multicultural and lively keynotes have inspired audiences from Australia, Denmark, Hong Kong, The Netherlands, New Zealand, and Singapore, to the United Kingdom and the United States.

He is the author of four books on international business and leadership, including the Amazon bestsellers *Bamboo Strong: Cultural Intelligence Secrets To Succeed In The New Global Economy* (2016), *The Master Key to Asia* (2013), and *The Master Key to China* (2014).

After living for twenty-five years in Italy, Switzerland, Hong Kong, Japan, South Korea, the United Kingdom, and the United States, he is now based in London, where he lives with his husband.

Find out more and connect with David via his website: **http://www.davidcliveprice.com**

APPENDIX

CULTURAL INTELLIGENCE (CQ) ASSESSMENT

The following is a brief introduction to cultural intelligence to help you answer the questions in the self-assessment and interpret your scores with the aim of raising your CQ to higher levels of performance. If you completed the first part of the Assessment (CQ Drive) in Chapter 5, note your score and then move on to the remaining sections. You will need to add all your scores together to achieve a full picture.

Further copies available at **http://davidcliveprice.com/ planner**

INTRODUCTION TO CULTURAL INTELLIGENCE

Cultural Intelligence (CQ) is the capability to relate and work effectively across cultures. It is based on years of scholarly research undertaken by academics globally spearheaded by the Cultural Intelligence Center in the US and Nanyang Business School in Singapore.

Business leaders, multicultural teams, international negotiators and other global executives in many sectors are adopting cultural intelligence as a key element of their personal and business growth.

Cultural intelligence is more than a methodology for registering cultural differences. It's a proven system to enhance your ability to communicate, network, negotiate and lead in culturally diverse workplaces across our globalised world—including virtual teams.

When we work within our own cultures and with people from familiar backgrounds, we have a wealth of shared experience and assumptions (often unconscious) that allow us to order and interpret what we encounter and observe. We know how to behave and 'do things properly'.

However, when interacting with people from different cultures and backgrounds, our familiar patterns of thinking and doing may not have the outcomes we expect. When we ask a direct question, for example, we may be puzzled or even annoyed that we don't receive a direct yes or no. We might not receive any answer at all.

This is why developing cultural intelligence is so important. CQ helps us to perform effectively in the multicultural workplace and overseas. It is a leadership capability that can be nurtured, measured and developed.

Whether opening up new markets, adapting global business models for local markets, serving customers across a number of cultures or negotiating across borders, cultural intelligence can make all the difference to your performance.

SO WHAT IS CULTURAL INTELLIGENCE?

Essentially, cultural intelligence consists of four inter-related capabilities (drive, knowledge, strategy, and action), each of which supports your overall CQ.

To discover more about each of the four capabilities and your effectiveness in each one, answer the self-assessment questions below each capability and add up the points you scored at the end.

Try not to look at the points system until you have finished answering the questions (it's on a separate page). Knowing which answer scores higher or lower will affect your choices and make the assessment invalid.

Remember: this is not a test and there are no right or wrong answers. The aim of the assessment is for you to gain an objective view of how well you might perform in multicultural encounters, or how you might develop your abilities further.

Rather than second-guessing the answers to achieve a 'higher' score, or being excessively modest, focus on giving honest answers that will increase your self-awareness. You will then have more confidence to create or revise your CQ Action Plan and you will give a more accurate picture of your leadership potential if you choose the **CQ Coaching Report** and **CQ Coaching Debrief.**

To obtain more effective results, work together with a partner or colleague or several colleagues (you can share or print out more sets of questionnaires). Have your partner mark your answers **with an asterisk *** and then exchange roles. Then move on to **Interpreting Your CQ Self-Assessment**.

If you choose the option of a **CQ Coaching Report** and **CQ Coaching Debrief**, remember to mark your answers **with an asterisk *** on the document before you send it off to info@davidcliveprice.com.

Further copies are available at http://davidcliveprice.com/planner

CQ-DRIVE

Courage

CQ Drive is your motivation and readiness to collaborate with others in a wide spectrum of cultural settings. It focuses on your ability to gain enjoyment from and reap the benefits of cross-cultural challenges in many contexts.

Considering culture and cultural diversity in a broad sense, please answer the following questions to assess your CQ Drive.

A. If you were asked to work in another culture or country, would you
1.   Pass up the opportunity if possible?

2.   Find out about the expatriate life and conditions?

3.   Google some information on the local culture, food, and customs?

4.   Ask a colleague's advice who has worked in that country?

B. When asked out to dinner by a foreign client or contact to a restaurant with 'exotic' food, do you:
1.   Try a little of everything at the host's suggestion?

2.   Order something very familiar from the menu?

3.   Try only those dishes that look attractive?

4.   Claim that your doctor will not allow you certain foods?

C. If you are going on holiday to or visiting a new country, do you:
1.   Learn some basic polite phrases in the local language?

2.   Get ready to speak slowly and clearly to be understood?

3.   Take along a translation app on your smart device or phone?

4.   Aim only to visit the 'international' areas?

D. When you are together with a person from a different culture, do you:
1.   Find out a little about their background and try to connect?

2.   Plan your conversation topics beforehand?

3.   Just act naturally and hope it all falls into place?

4.   Focus on listening to find common ground?

E. When you travel to other countries and cultures, do you:
1.   Look for signs in your native language and people who speak that language?

2.   Try to read some signs in a foreign language and find local people?

3.   Stick to guided tours with an interpreter and guide?

4.   Find your own interpreter and guide?

F. If you find yourself in a side alley in a new city with no signs, do you:

1. Look for the nearest route back to the main street?

2. Keep moving in the hope you will get to a public space?

3. Stop and look around for interesting sights and sounds?

4. Knock on the nearest door and ask for directions in English?

G.   If you are asked to participate in a local ritual or festival abroad, do you:

1. Refuse saying you are new to this country and its customs?

2. Watch what the other participants are doing and imitate them?

3. Ask a local what it means and if you can participate?

4. Go with the flow and see what happens next?

H.   When finding out about a new culture, do you:

1. Download a movie, novel, travel book or other guide to that culture?

2. Research items on the news media about that country?

3. Make friends with people from that culture in your home country?

4. See what interests, sports, or hobbies you have in common with that culture?

I.   On the first evening you arrive in a foreign country, do you:

1. Take a little walk outside the hotel or office perimeter to get acclimatized?

2. Go as far as possible into the locality searching for new experiences?

3. Get your bearings from the hotel concierge, local TV, or office manager?

4. Go to bed early and face the next day refreshed?

J. In your first week in a foreign country, do you:

1. Spend as much time as possible in familiar surroundings such as the hotel pool or international restaurants?

2. Look for ways to get off the beaten track and get adopted by a local friend or family?

3. Hang out for safety's sake with people like yourself?

4. Give yourself some specific challenges to enter the local culture step by step?

CQ KNOWLEDGE

Exploration

CQ Knowledge is the extent to which you understand how some cultures are similar to your own and how others are different. This involves knowledge of business and legal systems, family and social values, religious beliefs, as well as rules for verbal and nonverbal behaviour.

Considering culture and cultural diversity in a broad sense, please answer the following questions to assess your CQ Drive.

A. When meeting people from other cultures, do you:
1. Assume that they are just like you except with a few different customs?

2. Think you have to be careful because they are probably very different to you?

3. Listen and observe before making assumptions?

4. Behave as usual because you think your culture is the gold standard?

B. If you are announcing decisions in a foreign country or to a counterpart from another culture, do you:
1. State your position quite straightforwardly and expect the other side to be equally frank?

2. Choose a discreet time and a place to communicate your decisions?

3. Find a local partner or colleague to relay your decision in an appropriate way?

4. Hold back your decision until you are out of the country or environment?

C. If you were marketing a product in a new or unfamiliar market, would you:
1. Emphasize the global success of your product and sell it without any changes?
2. Research exactly what the local market and consumers like?
3. Spend some time in that country to discover local tastes and make friendships?
4. Find a distributor and expect them to adapt the product if really necessary?

D. When you see a movie or art or read books from other cultures, do you:
1. Identify mainly with what is known from your own background and values?
2. Wonder about the cultural differences but dismiss them with a shrug?
3. Find yourself trying out other viewpoints to your usual one?
4. Simply admire the diversity of imagination and art in other cultures?

E. When watching cookery competitions and cuisine programmes on television, do you:
1. Wonder where all the different ingredients come from and how they taste?
2. Imagine yourself making an exotic dish with similar ingredients?
3. Take one look at some exotic dishes and think how very unappealing they are?

4. Only pay attention to those dishes that are familiar to you from your own experience?

F. If you are spoken to in a foreign language and cannot communicate in your own language, do you:
1.Give up the conversation with an apology and say you don't understand?

2.Try to isolate some common words where you can understand each other with the help of sign language?

3.Carefully watch the facial and body language of your counterpart to interpret what they mean?

4.Speak slowly and loudly in your own language with repetitions?

G. If you need to deal with people of a certain nationality on a regular basis, do you:
1. Think of common values their culture might share with yours?

2. Approach them with caution because of what they are 'famous for' (inscrutability, precision, frankness etc.)?

3. Treat each person as an individual without preconceptions?

4. Wait for their national characteristics to reveal themselves and feel relieved you knew what to expect?

H. When you think about your own cultural identity, do you:
1. Feel proud that you continue to be aligned with your cultural background?

2. Wonder if adapting to other cultures has weakened your cultural identity?

3. Feel glad that you have rejected your cultural background in preference for being a 'global citizen'?

4. Have largely neutral feelings of what your culture means to you?

I. To obtain information about an item in the world news, do you:

1. Read your favourite newspaper or watch your regular news channel?

2. Read or watch a variety of news channels with differing views and audiences?

3. Go to a news channel in another language and listen to or watch the translation?

4. Google the story on your phone or smart device?

J. If you need professional guidance for a sport, hobby or overseas business venture, do you:

1. Find out what other people have done and follow their example?

2. Look for a source of inside knowledge, such as a retired professional, ex-player, expatriate or local?

3. Consult as many books and guides as possible?

4. Appoint an expert mentor or guide to give you regular support, advice, and accountability?

CQ STRATEGY

Perspective

CQ Strategy is an ability to be aware of what's happening in a cross-cultural encounter and to **plan** effectively on the basis of your understanding to implement knowledge and new ideas.

Considering culture and cultural diversity in a broad sense, please answer the following questions to assess your CQ Drive.

A. When travelling in a foreign country for the first time, do you:
  1. Search for clues about the culture and quickly draw conclusions?

  2. Wait to see what the clues might mean as a situation unfolds?

  3. Rely on what you have been told and ignore evidence to the contrary?

  4. Read as much as possible and rely on that for guidance?

B. When faced with a new cultural situation or inconvenience, do you:
  1. Immediately think 'that's not right, it shouldn't be like that'?

  2. Ask yourself why the situation is like that?

  3. Stand back a moment and take a big breath?

  4. Begin complaining until the situation is remedied to your satisfaction?

C. If you encounter a number of cross-cultural challenges every day, do you:

    1.   Play it by ear and hope you get better at it as you go along?

    2.   Find a moment at the end of the day to write down your observations and experiences?

    3.   Find the nearest friendly local and ask them about your questions?

    4.   Just go to the nearest bar or coffee shop and try to forget all about what's happened?

D. If you feel exhausted or stressed in an unfamiliar location, do you:

    1.   Go back to your apartment or hotel, lock the door and phone home?

    2.   Seek out some quiet place in nature or in a meditative setting to reflect?

    3.   Look for some diverting company for drinks and dinner?

    4.   Find some activity that allows you to slow down, relax and focus?

E. When you are preparing yourself for new cultural encounters or opportunities, do you:

    1.   Hope that your good instincts and energy will get you through?

    2.   Create a checklist or outline of what you will need from previous experiences?

    3.   Record some notes to yourself on your devices or laptop?

    4.   Write out a full-scale plan of what you intend to do and achieve?

F. When you encounter obstacles or difficulties in your plan (mental or written), do you:

1. Carry on regardless and try to bend the situation to your will?

2. Start mentally revising your plan in your head but not reveal what you are thinking?

3. Revise your plan both in your head and in the next steps you take?

4. Shrug your shoulders and decide it's best to let things take their course?

G. If you feel puzzled or suspicious of the way a cross-cultural encounter is unfolding, do you:

1. Become alarmed and put up your defenses?

2. Ask yourself why the situation is like it is and what might be going on?

3. Press on with questions that you know will confirm your suspicions?

4. Put yourself in the other person's position and imagine what they might be thinking?

H. When you set out in a new culture or experience a new country, do you:

1. Have highly optimistic expectations of your experience?

2. Expect things will turn out not very well and you will need help?

3. Know that there will be positives and negatives but the important thing is to have confidence?

4. Set your expectations at a reasonable level and learn from day to day?

I. When you are at an international event or conference with people from many countries, do you:

1. Stick to the people with the same background as yourself?

2. Try to interact casually with those of different cultures?

3. Try to interact with prepared topics with those of different cultures?

4. Choose the most difficult national circle to penetrate and go in with a couple of phrases in their language?

J. If you are about to enter a new cross-cultural situation do you:

1. Ask yourself what you expect to happen?

2. Don't think much about it and trust to the flow?

3. Examine your biggest fears and biggest hopes?

4. Follow what others are doing and do the same?

CQ ACTION

Performance

CQ Action focuses on the appropriate verbal and physical behaviour for diverse cross-cultural situations. It develops your ability to 'flex' mentally, to avoid miscommunication, and to create trust.

Considering culture and cultural diversity in a broad sense, please answer the following questions to assess your CQ Drive.

A. If you are visiting a new country or market to do business, do you:

1. Learn as much etiquette in as short a time as possible?

2. Ignore etiquette and simply do what other non-locals do?

3. Try a halfway house between observing some etiquette rules and being yourself?

4. Get a complete crash course in behaviour from a local or expatriate?

B. If you go out to dinner with local people in a new culture, do you:

1. Talk about business as soon as the dishes arrive?

2. Talk about family, friends, hobbies and interests?

3. Adjust your dinner conversation to topics your hosts feel comfortable with?

4. Ignore any conventions, have a few drinks and talk about anything that you like?

C. When interacting with people from a different culture, do you:
1. Adapt your communication style to the way they speak?

2. Assume they will understand you in English because it is a common language around the world?

3. Try to express yourself with the same body language and gestures they use?

4. Repeat yourself often so that they really understand what you mean?

D. When exploring a new country or a new work assignment overseas, do you:
1. Learn and practise some basic phrases of the local language to get you around?

2. Sign up for a beginners' language course?

3. Hope that you can get by with English and a translation app?

4. Always have a local nearby who can translate for you when necessary?

E. When travelling in other countries around the world, do you:
1. Get what you want by speaking loudly in English?

2. Speak quietly and smile a lot to get what you want?

3. Listen to local conversations and watch how locals express themselves?

4. Adapt your intonation in English and/or local language to local sounds and body language?

F.   If you had to give a presentation to an audience from another culture or many cultures, would you:

   1.   Be as natural and authentic as possible using your command of the English language?

   2.   Slow down the way you speak, leave adequate pauses, and use short sentences?

   3.   Rely on your slides to get your message across to anyone who doesn't follow?

   4.   Research your audience beforehand and see what style of English (or French or Spanish) would appeal to most people?

G.   If you had a choice between working with a multicultural team and people of your own background, would you:

   1.   Prefer to work with people of your own background?

   2.   Prefer to work with a mix of people who are similar to you and those from different backgrounds?

   3.   Not really mind either way?

   4.   Choose a multicultural team every time because of the gains in creative thinking?

H.   If somebody from another culture does not give you a straightforward decision on a business matter, do you:

   1.   Assume this is to avoid being tied down to a contract or obligation?

   2.   Assume they have not understood the situation clearly and ask again?

   3.   Consider ways to reframe the question that avoid a direct response?

4. Consider the decision in the context of many possible ways to build the relationship?

I. If you develop your CQ by experiencing different cross-cultural situations, do you:
1. Look for ways to share your expertise with others in your life and organisation?

2. Keep your discoveries to yourself as a form of competitive advantage?

3. Continue to test your discoveries in new cultural encounters and share them with others?

4. Consider your discoveries as interesting but not important in your life or business?

J. When considering the level of your cultural intelligence, do you:
1. Plan to develop it further but only on an occasional basis?

2. Look to develop it further by creating and implementing a CQ Plan for your life and business?

3. Decide to create a CQ Plan for your business or organisation and implement it together with a mentor or guide?

4. Hope your cultural intelligence gets better with some hit-and-miss experiences?

INTERPRETING YOUR CQ
SELF-ASSESSMENT

Circle the answer number you chose for each CQ factor and set of questions. Input your score for that answer and then add up the scores according to your answers to reach an overall total.

CQ Drive (Courage) You Scored (input your score for each set of questions below)

    A.
    1 = 1, 2 = 2, 3 = 3, 4 = 4
    B.
    1 = 4, 2 = 3, 3 = 2, 4 = 1
    C.
    1 = 4, 2 = 2, 3 = 3, 4 = 1
    D.
    1 = 3, 2 = 2, 3 = 1, 4 = 4
    E.
    1 = 1, 2 = 4, 3 = 2, 4 = 3
    F.
    1 = 1, 2 = 2, 3 = 4, 4 = 3
    G.
    1 = 1, 2 = 3, 3 = 4, 4 = 2
    H.
    1 = 2, 2 = 1, 3 = 4, 4 = 3
    I.
    1 = 3, 2 = 4, 3 = 2, 1 = 1
    J.
    1 = 2, 2 = 4, 3 = 1, 4 = 3

Your CQ Drive Total Points =

CQ Knowledge (Exploration)You Scored (input your score for each set of questions below)

A.
1 = 3,2 = 2,3 = 4, 4 = 1
B.
1 = 2, 2 = 3, 3 = 4, 4 = 1
C.
1 = 1, 2 = 3, 3 = 4,4 = 2
D.
1 = 2, 2 = 1,3 = 4,4 = 3
E.
1 = 3, 2 = 4, 3 = 1, 4 = 2
F.
1 = 1,2 = 4, 3 = 3, 4 = 2
G.
1 = 3, 2 = 2, 3 = 4, 4 = 1
H.
1 = 4, 2 = 3, 3 = 1,4 = 2
I.
1 = 1, 2 = 4, 3 = 3, 4 = 2
J.
1 = 1, 2 = 3, 3 = 2, 4 = 4

Your CQ Knowledge Total Points =

CQ Strategy (Perspective)You Scored (input your score for each set of questions below)

A.
1 = 2, 2 = 4, 3 = 1, 4 = 3
B.
1 = 2, 2 = 4, 3 = 3, 4 = 1
C.
1 = 2, 2 = 3, 3 = 4, 4 = 1
D.
1 = 1, 2 = 4, 3 = 2, 4 = 3
E.
1 = 1, 2 = 3, 3 = 2, 4 = 4
F.
1 = 1, 2 = 3, 3 = 4, 4 = 2
G.
1 = 1, 2 = 3, 3 = 2, 4 = 4
H.
1 = 2, 2 = 1, 3 = 3, 4 = 4
I.
1 = 1, 2 = 2, 3 = 3, 4 = 4
J.
1 = 4, 2 = 1, 3 = 3, 4 = 2

Your CQ Strategy Total Points =

CQ Action (Performance) You Scored (input your score for each set of questions below)

A.
1 = 2, 2 = 1, 3 = 4, 4 = 3
B.
1 = 2, 2 = 3, 3 = 4, 4 = 1
C.
1 = 4, 2 = 2, 3 = 3, 4 = 1
D.
1 = 4, 2 = 3, 3 = 1, 4 = 2
E.
1 = 1, 2 = 2, 3 = 3, 4 = 4
F.
1 = 2, 2 = 3, 3 = 1, 4 = 4
G.
1 = 1, 2 = 3, 3 = 2, 4 = 4
H.
1 = 2, 2 = 1, 3 = 3, 4 = 4
I.
1 = 3, 2 = 2, 3 = 4, 4 = 1
J.
1 = 2, 2 = 3, 3 = 4, 4 = 1

Your CQ Action Total Points =

Congratulations you've finished the scoring section!

Your TOTAL CQ POINTS
(out of a possible 160 points) =

OVERALL SCORES

Score: *120-160* High CQ development and executive maturity

Score: *80-120* High average CQ development and executive maturity

Score: *40-80* Average CQ development and executive maturity

Remember there is no top and bottom of the class for CQ development. All of us have the capability within us to become Bamboo Leaders with a high degree of cultural intelligence and executive maturity.

It all depends how motivated you are to draw out those intercultural skills that we have within us. Some of us have far more CQ Knowledge that we have CQ Drive; others have more developed CQ Strategy than we have CQ Action.

No one has reached perfection in any of the capabilities, far less achieved a perfect combination of all four interdependent factors. Your capacity for success lies entirely within yourself.

Once you complete the next section, you are ready for your optional CQ Coaching Report and CQ Coaching Debrief!

NEXT STEP: CREATING A CQ ACTION PLAN

The primary aim of the CQ Leadership Assessment & Development Tool is to make you more conscious of your current strengths and weakness when dealing with culturally diverse situations and people, and to encourage you to develop your CQ capabilities and leadership skills going forward.

We suggest you take time to reflect on your answers in the CQ Leadership Assessment, and also to consider how you might create a **CQ Action Plan**, both to strengthen your performance as a leader and enhance your personal development.

We will help you to interpret your results and to choose specific strategies, insights and goals that you can action NOW rather than in some distant future to develop your global leadership skills.

1. Write down how you think you rate on your overall CQ.

2. Which of the four CQ capabilities do you feel strongest in?

3. Give THREE reasons why this capability is stronger than the others.

    a.

    b.

    c.

4. Which of your CQ capabilities need to be developed more?

5. Did you discover anything special or surprising about your CQ capabilities?

6. Why do you think this discovery is special or surprising?

7. List FOUR ways you could use these strengths to develop your other capabilities.

    a.

    b.

    c.

    d.

8. Choose ONE of these ways to implement in the next WEEK.

NEXT STEP: IMPLEMENTING YOUR CQ ACTION PLAN

Now you are ready to implement your **CQ Plan of Action** with specific steps, and to review progress and accountability on a regular basis. What steps will you take next?

In addition to the CQ Leadership Assessment, most clients request additional support with their CQ Action Plan. This includes **David Clive Price** himself:

- Interpreting your CQ Leadership Assessment results and writing a **CQ Coaching Report** that focuses on key leadership and cultural intelligence strengths, as well as potential for improvement and personal development recommendations

- Our team scheduling a 1-hour **CQ Coaching Debrief** with you so David can fully explain and review your CQ Report in detail and discuss the leadership development strategy he has prepared for you.

Note: Organisations that engage David for Bamboo Leader Workshops/Retreats that are half-day or longer, receive a complimentary **CQ Assessment** for each attendee.

If you want more help to put into action your CQ Plan, request a CQ Coaching Report or schedule a CQ Coaching Debrief, contact us at info@davdicliveprice.com **or call +44 (0) 7766335805.**

COURSES AND CERTIFICATIONS

Global DISC™ Certification

Leveraging personal and cultural differences

Due to the rise of technology and the information age most organisations compete based primarily on their people. The ability to recruit, engage, and retain quality employees is the most challenging and expensive priority.

In today's fast-moving, complex organisations, 90 percent of execution is interaction between people who think and behave differently. The skill to turn those differences into synergy instead of painful liability is the key to remain competitive.

The people challenges of globalisation cannot be solved using solutions created in the last century. Unfortunately, that is what 99 per cent of companies buy and sell today.

Cultural Intelligence (ICQ) is an often misunderstood concept as most people when they hear 'intercultural' think 'international'. However, in reality it means 'interpersonal'. If a company serves or employs more than one person, they are already multicultural, even if they are not multinational.

60-80 per cent of all difficulties in organisations stem from strained relationships between employees, not from deficits in an individual employee's skill or motivation.

Top 3 causes of workplace conflict:
1. Personality clashes
2. Poor leadership
3. Clashing values

Global DISC™ addresses all 3 of them.

The programme is designed for trainers and coaches who would like to stand out from the crowd by offering the latest, multi award-winning solution to their clients whose performance depends on how well they get on with the individual they are dealing with.

It is also available as corporate training for senior leaders, managers, sales, and customer service professionals who want to minimise the interaction gap in their team or bridge the intercultural gap with their clients and colleagues.

The Global DISC™ Certification is accredited by the International Coaching Federation (ICF) and approved for 10 Coaching Continuation Education (CCE's) Units.

Contact:
Csaba@ICQ.global
David@davidcliveprice.com

'Global DISC™ is a powerful tool for Intelligent Leaders to leverage personal and cultural differences for competitive advantage, to enable trust and to build high-performing teams at home and globally.'

John Mattone, the number one authority on Intelligent Leadership and the world's top executive coach, Steve Jobs' former coach

'ICQ Global delivered a great interactive presentation to BBC managers about cultural intelligence for leadership. BBC is a global and multicultural broadcaster so in order to be an effective organisation we need to have good cultural intelligence (ICQ). Global DISC gave us the know-how and tools to be able to achieve this.'

Toby Mildon, Inclusion and Diversity Lead for BBC Design & Engineering, Finance & Operations and Radio

EXECUTIVE COACHING CERTIFICATION – INTELLIGENT LEADERSHIP™

A 3-Day Immersive Online Journey in Executive Leadership Coach Development

Executive coaching certification under John Mattone's *Intelligent Leadership Programme* is a compelling opportunity to grow your business and brand as a leading executive coach by offering your clients a proven executive coaching process and unique leadership coach development tools guaranteed to produce results and a powerful ROI. Discover the unique and powerful components of the Intelligent Leadership (IL) Executive Coaching Blueprint created and mastered by John Mattone, the world's number one authority on corporate culture and leadership and the former coach to Steve Jobs. Now you can become certified in this unique executive coaching process made famous by John Mattone.

The Intelligent Leadership™ Executive Coaching 'Initial Mastery' Certification is accredited by the International Coach Federation (ICF) and approved for 22.25 Coaching Continuation Education (CCE's) Units AND 21.75 Core Credits!

The John Mattone Intelligent Leadership (IL) Executive Coaching Certification Programme is a 3-day 'immersive' journey in executive and leadership coach development. Ultimately, this comprehensive programme enables external and internal coaches to help leaders and future leaders unlock and unleash their potential so they truly become the best leaders and people they can be. The IL Executive Coaching Process achieves this by igniting and strengthening a leaders inner-core and outer-core, which enables them to realize 4 'game-changing' outcomes that they can leverage as leaders in their business and life: *altruism, affiliation, achievement,* and a*bundance* (The 4 A's). The 4 A's are the seeds to achieving sustained greatness and creating a lasting legacy. This programme includes participating in an 'immersive' 3-day hands-on learning experience (also available online) with John Mattone himself or Master Certified Coach David Clive Price; an extensive 600-page Coaches Resource Manual; and an optional but highly recommended two-year development journey guaranteed to help the certified IL coach grow their coaching skills as well as their success as a coach.

Becoming initially certified in the IL Executive Coaching Process (Level I) certifies and enables the coach to carry out coaching assignments using the IL Process. However, the goal is for each coach to reach Level II 'Advanced IL Executive Coach' and Level III 'Master IL Executive Coach' within two years from the time they are awarded the 'Initial Mastery' IL Certification.

For more information on the requirements for achieving each level, and on the Intelligent Leadership Executive Coaching Process, visit:

http://johnmattone.com
http://davidcliveprice.com/coaching

Since 2015, the research organisation, Globalgurus.org, has ranked John Mattone as one of the world's top leadership authorities and speakers. In 2015, John Mattone's Intelligent Leadership™ was named as one of the three Top Advanced Leadership Development Programs that Change Lives.

INTELLIGENT GLOBAL LEADERSHIP™ CERTIFICATION

The competitive advantage to bring out the best in diverse teams through Intelligent Global Leadership in a volatile, uncertain, complex, and ambiguous world

A multi-award winning, one and a half day certification and training programme to bring out the best in leaders and teams through the highest level of cultural intelligence.

The combination of Global DISC™, Bamboo Leadership, and the Intelligent Leadership model created by John Mattone is the competitive advantage to showcase your expertise in a fast-paced, multicultural world.

The programme includes the Intelligent Global Leadership slides, 30 Global DISC™ assessment codes, Dr David Clive Price's *Bamboo Strong* and *The Age of Pluralism* books, and six hours pre-work.

The Intelligent Global Leadership™ Certification is accredited by the International Coaching Federation (ICF) and approved for 18 Coaching Continuation Education (CCE's) Units (7 Core Credits and 11 Resource Development Credits).

INTELLIGENT GLOBAL LEADERSHIP™ — MASTER COACH CERTIFICATION

A multi-award winning, immersive three-day certification and training programme to develop the highest possible levels of executive coaching combined with global mindset and leadership.

The combination of Global DISC™, Bamboo Leadership, and the Intelligent Leadership model created by John Mattone is the competitive advantage to radically transform your expertise in a fast-paced, multicultural world.

The programme includes the Intelligent Global Leadership slides (to facilitate training with others), 30 Global DISC™ assessment codes, the *Bamboo Strong* and John Mattone's *Intelligent Leadership* books, a 600-page Coaches Resource Manual created by John Mattone, and six hours pre-work.

The Intelligent Global Leadership™ – Master Coach Certification is accredited by the International Coaching Federation (ICF) and approved for 40 Coaching Continuation Education (CCE's) Units, including Global DISC, Bamboo Leadership and Intelligent Leadership.

INTELLIGENT GLOBAL LEADERSHIP™ — MASTERMIND AND EXECUTIVE COACHING

The competitive advantage to bring out the best in diverse teams through Intelligent Global Leadership in a volatile, uncertain, complex, and ambiguous world.

The Intelligent Global Leadership programme is offered as a six-month Mastermind for select groups of senior executives, with a half-day Mastermind per month.

The combination of Global DISC™, Bamboo Leadership, and the Intelligent Leadership™ model forms the basis of personalised, intensive 1-2-1 executive coaching over six to nine months.

For More News About David Clive Price,
Signup For Our Newsletter:

http://wbp.bz/newsletter

Word-of-mouth is critical to an author's long-term success. If you appreciated this book please leave a review on the Amazon sales page:

http://wbp.bz/aopa

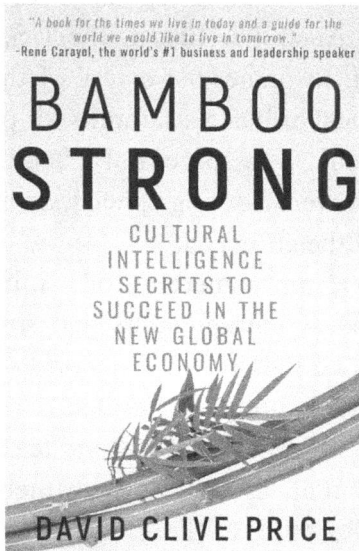
BECOMING A BAMBOO LEADER

We are all on a CQ journey every day of our lives in this rich, complex, and sometimes deeply unsettling world. In our businesses, families, and relationships, we connect as a matter of course with people from every culture. I am by no means different in talking regularly via Skype to clients and contacts in Australia, Brazil, the US, France, Japan, and Hong Kong, to name just a few of the countries and locations. Whether for business, family, or pleasure, I get on a plane to Denmark, Singapore, Italy, South Korea, or even Myanmar as if it were nothing special, as if the destination were just around the corner.

In this sense I am something of a mini-multinational, just like millions of entrepreneurs and small or medium-size businesses like me around the world—and millions of tourists too. Even at home in London, I interact regularly with different members of multicultural teams in companies both large and small, as well as with their corresponding teams in countries all over the globe. Almost everything I do involves some kind of cross-cultural element. I exercise three times a week at my local gym by the River Thames in a BODYPUMP class where it only recently occurred to me to count how many nationalities were in the studio.

The result astounded me. I discovered that I take regular exercise with BODYPUMPers of around thirty-five nations, of which just two 'locally grown' fitness fanatics (including myself) represent the UK. Our instructors are Brazilian, Cypriot, Hong Kong Chinese, and Latvian. And yet, until I did my little study—which eased the pain of the countless lower-half lunges—it did not occur to me that there was anything special in our thrice-weekly cultural mash-up. Or rather, it occurred to me on some level where my cultural intelligence was on automatic—the space where I translated what was said to me in different versions of English, with a few Portuguese or Greek words thrown in, and where I instinctively modulated my own Cambridge English to chime with different ways of speaking the language.

In other words, my BODYPUMP class is a microcosm of what I have trained my CQ to do over the past forty years: tune in, accept, interpret, respond with similar intonation and even choice of words, harmonize, gain trust, make friendships, gain benefits.

I don't know whether this strikes a chord with you or not. It's only a simple example, but I'm sure if you think over your daily routine in your workplace or at home, you might come up with similar examples of almost unnoticed adapting or, as some of the CQ studies call it, 'flexing'. It may be the way you talk with your local corner shop owner on the way to work, or the regulars at your coffee shop, or colleagues on your team, or your boss. It's something we do in the face of the incredible diversity of our world, both in the workplace and when communicating via virtual networks. We try to get on the other person's wavelength.

We may not be very good at it. We may have little experience of it. We may be better with understanding and adapting to some cultures rather than others. But I think, if you go deep inside, you will catch glimpses of moments when this reaching out or flexing, or whatever you want to call it, really worked for you. A moment of much deeper understanding. A moment of curiosity crowned with a flash of enlightenment. A moment of greater tolerance, or compassion, or simply human warmth. A moment when you bridged that gap with a person from another background almost without thinking—and yet retained the essential being that is you, with all your values and beliefs intact.

I call a person who regularly achieves this level of understanding and flexibility a Bamboo Leader. The bamboo bends in the wind, but it is inherently very strong. It is still used for scaffolding in some parts of the world. It flexes with wind, and rain, and even snow but always springs back.

It has an empty centre with space to be filled.

In other words, the bamboo presents both empathy and strength. As the world becomes more multipolar, more connected, and more multicultural, we need to develop the qualities of the Bamboo Leader in ourselves. That is the journey I'd like to guide you on in this book—a journey to becoming more Bamboo Strong in today's global economy.

DO YOU SPEAK SWISS GERMAN ?

When I talk about a 'cultural intelligence journey', I don't mean that we are all more or less passengers bound in the same direction as soon as we consciously step on the CQ Express—and that we're all going to end up at the same destination once we have crossed similar mountains, and rivers, and national borders, and cultural barriers.

We all respond differently to the challenges of this complex, cross-cultural world of ours, and each one of us is different and individual. We will have personal and individual reactions to different cultural settings and scenarios. It is by no means certain where we will end up even when we have developed our cultural intelligence over many years and in many different situations. Your CQ Express might take you anywhere.

For some people—and these tend to be the majority— it is extremely difficult to function successfully when confronted with cultures and attitudes that are not very similar to their own. Even when they are posted to other countries in their jobs, they often fail to adapt to the prevailing culture or to even set foot outside their own safe expatriate ghetto. They want everyone they encounter to be 'just like me' and to do things 'just like at home'. And when that doesn't work out for them, they complain to their expatriate colleagues that they don't 'get' the Chinese, or the Brazilians, or the Indians.

They want a system that will enable them to interact safely with the locals, or people from the same region, without having to make any adjustments in their values or behaviour. Lists of dos and don'ts are often the main support that such professionals use (if they use any), as if a quick rundown of etiquette tips will save them the painful business of overcoming cultural differences and communicating effectively.

This shopping list approach to cultural adjustment is perhaps better than making no effort at all. However, it is unlikely to work when you are confronted (as we all are, sometimes several times a day) by a multiplicity of different cultural situations—ethnic, generational, or organizational. How do you handle the East Asia portfolio of clients you have been handed when you are told the Japanese are different to the South Koreans, who are different to the Mainland Chinese, who are different to the Taiwanese? How do you avoid stereotypes when you rely on your etiquette tips and shopping lists? How do you treat a Japanese-American differently to a Tokyo-born Japanese?

Don't get me wrong. A list is an attempt at understanding or fitting in, but it won't help you respond effectively to a variety of cultural contexts. You will become confused when trying to remember what to do when and in what culture. You will get cultural overload, and you will do what many stressed people do: say it's all a waste of time, stick to your guns, and not bother.

This is a great shame because with a little help to flex your cultural muscles, you could end up like I have in my BODYPUMP class. You could instinctively adjust to different peoples from different cultures almost without noticing you are doing it. After the class is over, I spend some time exchanging a few words in Italian with Fabrizio, the barista at the club's coffee bar. Fabrizio clearly enjoys these little chats and often offers me a salmon and salad panino on the house to accompany my double macchiato. It is not a premeditated ruse on my part. I don't have a list to tell me that Italians like hand gestures and exaggerated flattery. I just do what comes naturally. I try a little cultural intelligence and *voil*à*!* (Or rather, *ecco!)*

You might say that all this proves is that we should treat people as individuals. And you would be right. Beyond the cultural differences, we often find that people are the same all over the world. They have the same needs, and insecurities, and loves, and dreams that we have.

However, to discover and celebrate this, you have to make some effort to get on the same wavelength, to reach out and communicate, and above all to respect others' beliefs and traditions. Cultural intelligence, which also includes cultural sensitivity, helps you to do this.

In Switzerland, I discovered that speaking English did not make me a trusted member of my Swiss family, not even High German did. I had to speak Swiss German and *make the effort* to become accepted. If you take the example of Switzerland out into today's global economy, you will find that English being spoken almost everywhere does not mean that we are all more less the same and on the same wavelength. There are many local versions of English, all with their own dialect and expressions and meanings. English is also a second or perhaps a third language in vast areas of the planet. Your English is not necessarily my English. You are not me. Yes, we are living in an era of extraordinary innovation, convergence, and connectivity. However, the great paradox is that the more we are connected, and the smaller the world seems, the more we have to respond effectively to new markets and cultures that were previously hidden from us. We are virtually present now and sometimes physically present in Shanghai and Bangalore, in Yangon, and Sao Paolo. How do we grasp the opportunities? How do we communicate? How do we show the necessary respect and not come over as Neanderthals with an excess of arrogance?

If you want to succeed as a Bamboo Leader, you will have to speak the equivalent of some Swiss German in a world of English. You will have to relate, to listen, and to adapt, and only then will you develop the skills to successfully lead.

http://wbp.bz/bamboostronga

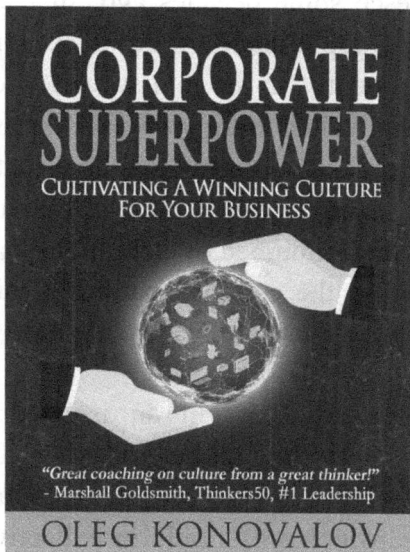
Chapter One

Live, Immaterial, and Functional

Since the time of Cicero, people have tended to take the phenomenon of culture for granted, often assuming that it is synonymous with organizational culture. However, a more specialized understanding of organizational culture began to coalesce some decades ago. In fact, it was first described as a group climate by Lewin, Lippitt, and White in 1939. Subsequently, in the mid-seventies, organizational norms, roles, and values were viewed in terms of the social psychology of organizations, although, at that stage, it was not explicitly stated as organizational climate or culture. Since then, a large number of definitions have appeared, serving to confirm the complex nature of this incorporeal being. However, we are still exploring this elephant in a dark room.

Culture does not exist in an isolated and purified environment without the presence of other people. Culture is a complex phenomenon, deeply interpenetrating all of our daily activities, which exists only in collectives of people, i.e. in states, nations, and organizations. Culture is a system itself. The word "system" derives from the ancient Greek word *systema* which comes from two words – *syn*, which means "together", and *histemi*, which means "to set." System is actually an idea which defines how process or ideology is to be set for the best possible performance or outcome. Cultural or ideological systems can be seen as a collection of roles which reflect human values and thus have a direct impact on organizational results. As a system, culture needs to be viewed using a systematic approach and not a mono-dimensional view.

Three Dimensions of Culture

Culture is multidimensional. One dimension is pragmatic and rational, regulating rules, norms, and codes of working in organizations. A second dimension is more irrational and incorporates the behavioral and psychological approach of the group's members to their duties and to the organization itself. A third dimension reflects the transcendent side of culture, which can be viewed as the organizational cathedral, the reference point for the entire organization's activity.

Regarding the strictly rational aspect, Aristotle wisely defined a state, as an interaction for reaching mutual goals. Not short-term tasks, but goals of successful survival, prosperity, mutual support, defense, and satisfaction of its own needs. Applying Aristotle's definition to an organizational viewpoint, we can say that it is similar to the purpose of the state, just on a smaller scale – an organization is the interaction of its members ordered to reach defined goals that benefit the organization.

Organisational Anatomy (Konovalov 2016, 71) defines organizational culture as a catalyzer of performance. I will use this definition in the present discussion as being the most advanced and practically relevant to the aims of all organizations. Looking at the spiritual or transcendent side, we can consider company culture as the soul of the organizational body, which helps the brain (management) motivate the body for action, sense the environment, attract stakeholders' positive emotions and energy, stimulate and encourage development, and drive the organization through tough times.

This third dimension is the dynamic power and spiritual core of the organization. It is built on symbols which shape the company's psychological state and define the boundaries of its influence. We will discuss the role of symbols and values in more detail later as this is a tremendously critical and under-appreciated issue.

Each of these facets of organizational culture empowers and enlightens the other sides of the immaterial core of any company, and by doing so, gives life and vitality to a company. Culture also defines the boundaries of an organization. Within those boundaries, dependent upon the culture's nature, the talents of the employees are revealed and allowed to flourish.

http://wbp.bz/csa

Introduction

"One of the greatest and simplest tools for learning more and growing is doing more." - Washington Irving

In 1993 I founded my software company 21st Century Technologies, Inc. I have since build custom database software systems for the top pharmaceutical and semiconductor companies in the world. Although I still build database software systems, my efforts have moved in the direction of building websites that increase companies sales and doing online marketing, search engine optimization and search engine marketing/pay per click advertising. This experience has led me to founding the publishing company WildBlue Press along with my partner Steve Jackson. I'm past CTO and founder of Mercury Leads along with my partners Paul Plvan and Tom Link, and I'm past CTO of Well.org.

In my marketing shoes I have increased a software product customer's sales from $500,000/year to $4,000,000/year, an 8-fold increase in sales. I increased an HVAC customer's sales by $400K in one month and I have helped countless customers establish, maintain and grow their online presence.

Efficiency and delivery of top-quality services in all of these endeavors is absolutely critical to the success of my companies, and more importantly my customers. I am always on the hunt for great tools that will improve the fruits of my labors and save me time.

In writing this eBook I have literally combed through my installed applications, paid services, daily routines and bookmarks (my bookmark manager is one of the tools) to make sure this list of productivity tools is complete. I have been thinking about doing it for years, now these tools are all here for you to incorporate into your own business and research efforts.

I have no doubt that you will find multiple tools here that will make your life, or the lives of your customers better and more efficient.

Productivity

Use Your Mind Offline

Although this is a technique more than a tool, it is my favorite productivity method to line up my ducks for the time that I make it to my desk for work. I work with many customers for my marketing company, and authors for my publishing company. I do marketing and take care of the websites as well as write books and take care of personal responsibilities. That means I always have a lot of balls that I'm juggling to keep in the air. Many of the tasks I am responsible for are important, if not critical, so I need to make sure they are all completed as required.

What I do to make sure I think of all of the most important tasks - is to get completely away from them all and do something I enjoy that removes me entirely from those very tasks. I find a quiet spot and get back to reading my latest favorite book. While my mind is immersed in the landscapes and characters of the book I'm reading, it is also subconsciously strolling through all that I'm involved in. Periodically a thought will fly by about one of my responsibilities, or maybe (and oftentimes) a great idea. I'll then pull up GMail on my phone or Kindle, make a note to myself and not send the email. I usually have ten or twenty items before I am done reading. When I move on to the rest of my day I send the email and when I'm back at my desk I manage all of this info on my desktop.

Using GMail and my devices is just how I do it. I sync GMail on my devices, so these emails can all be read on all of them. The analog version is to keep a pad of paper and a pen handy.

The biggest benefit of this is that I got some reading done. "I read and think," Warren Buffett once said. "So I do more reading and thinking, and make less impulse decisions than most people in business." (Marguerite Ward, "Warren Buffett's reading routine could make you smarter, science suggests", *http://www.cnbc.com/2016/11/16/warren-buffetts-reading-routine-could-make-you-smarter-suggests-science.html*, November 16, 2016)

Lookout Free Security App for Mobile Devices

https://www.lookout.com

This is the first app you should load onto your smart phone. Available for both the iOS and Android formats this security app performs multiple critical functions for you:

Scans all files and apps you download for viruses

Backs up your contacts

Can locate your device in case you lose it

Has a scream feature that you can invoke remotely

You need to have an account at lookout.com to access your backed up info or find your device after you have lost it. You can also set the device to scream so you can find it. The paid version ($3/month) has Safe Browsing security scans of the web pages you visit in your browser, allows you to lock or wipe the phone remotely and backs up your images.

Team Viewer Free Remote PC Control
https://www.teamviewer.us/

Control your desktop (or any other) pc from any mobile device with this free (for personal use) service. Instead of carrying your laptop everywhere, you can take your iPad or Kindle then access and control your main computer from anywhere. This is a real productivity tool that allows you to do your work immediately anywhere while you are reading your tablet device instead of taking a note and doing the work later.

http://wbp.bz/57toolsa

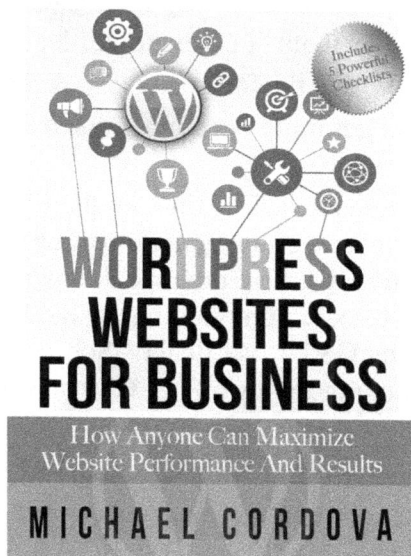
The Importance of Long-Tail Keywords, Intent and the Mobile Factor

When you use keyword phrases consisting of several words in them you have a much better chance of getting ranked for those keyword phrases. Not only that, you can incorporate the users intent in them. For example, let's say you were selling golf clubs. See the following keywords and note how the search terms get more specific and show more intent as you go down:

golf – Someone killing time on their computer

golf clubs – Someone doing general research for golf clubs

pitching wedge – Someone doing general research on pitching wedges

ping G30 driver deals – Someone looking to buy a Ping G30 driver

When doing your keyword research you need to think about what intent you are looking to capture, what specific types of products and services you *want to* provide. Of course it varies by the type of company. Here are some examples of long-tail keywords with intent to engage or purchase:

small business cpa firm to reduce our taxes

auto mechanic to fix my 2017 jeep grand cherokee transmission

chiropractor specializing in a stiff neck

whole roasted pig with green chile catering service (I must be getting hungry)

You need to keep the long-tail and intent concepts in mind when you do your keyword research and write your content. This refinement will make a huge difference in your results. In the above examples, if you instead had focused on cpa firm, auto mechanic, chiropractor or catering service then you'll not only *not be* targeting your company's specific services, but you'll be attempting to rank for keywords that are the most difficult to get top organic rankings for.

Now that we have really smart phones that you can just ask questions of like the Apple Siri or the Android "Ok Google…" capability, and devices like the Amazon Echo (Alexa) and Google Home, search engine queries are now being slanted to those coming from these devices. Now queries like these are becoming more important:

"Ok Google, what's the best Mexican restaurant near me?"

"Alexa, what are the best local activities for kids"

"What are the best local coffee shops"

People are searching on their mobile devices in a hands-free scenario looking for a service that they can use now. *They're on the way!* You need to think about these concepts when you compile your list of keywords that you'll be targeting for your website content.

The Best Tools to Find Long-Tail Keywords

Google again provides great methods and tools to acquire highly relevant long-tail keywords. Since it is Google rankings that you are after, taking Google's suggestions is getting your keywords straight from the horse's mouth.

Do a Google search for your topic and pay attention to the search terms that Google suggests in the search box:

auto insurance| 🔍

auto insurance
auto insurance **colorado**
auto insurance **quotes**
auto insurance **denver**
auto insurance **florida**
auto insurance **near me**
auto insurance **companies**
auto insurance **america**
auto insurance **comparison**
auto insurance **colorado springs**

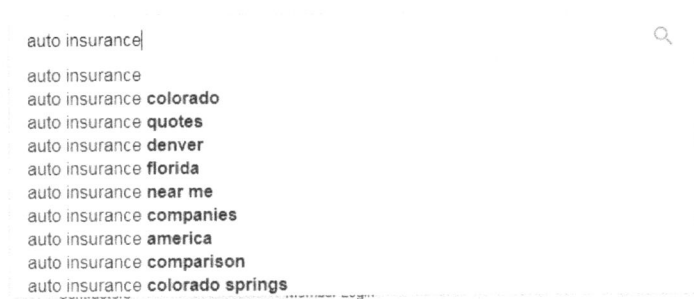

Next, scroll down to the bottom of the results of your search and note the other terms (long-tail keywords) that Google suggests for you:

Searches related to concrete contractor

concrete **contractors denver**	**commercial** concrete **contractors denver**
concrete **delivery denver**	**good day** concrete
residential concrete **denver**	**denver** concrete **prices**
denver concrete **services**	**sunny day** concrete

Grab the keyword phrases that are relevant to your current needs and use them in your article. If you need more then recycle - take the relevant ones and use them in another search to get more suggestions.

A favorite tool among marketers is UberSuggest.io. You just type in a seed keyword, and it gives you a ton of other keywords by appending words to your seed keyword starting with each letter of the alphabet. The video at the bottom of the page shows you how to copy and paste these keywords to a spreadsheet and use all of their basic functions.

Another quick source of long-tail keywords is http://soovle.com. Just type in your keyword and they'll list relevant options from Google, Bing, Yahoo!, Wikipedia, Youtube, Answers.com and Amazon.

Many more keyword tools are available in the free download that you can grab from the Resources section at the end of this book.

Use Qualified, Prioritized Keywords to Drive Compelling Content

Once you have completed the above, then you have the information you need to start mapping out your website content. Create a Wordpress category for each of the categories in the spreadsheet. If a category is too broad, then break it down into multiple categories of finer detail. Sort the spreadsheet by two columns - priority then category. This provides you with the keywords most relevant to your business and the topics (categories) that you can provide solutions for. Next create a list of solutions representing a series of posts for each of the categories. You don't have to write the content now, just a list of concepts/solutions that you'll write about. This list will be your content map for future blog posts. Think in terms of problems that your customers are looking to solve, and solutions that you have already provided or can provide.

Ask each member of your team to make a list of the solutions they have provided for customers, then drop each one into the most relevant category. Doing this will provide a great inventory of blog posts that are targeted to solving your customers problems with your company's priorities built-in. They'll be customer-centric in terms of solutions to their problems, and they'll be focusing on keywords that are a priority to your business with a great chance of getting rankings and traffic from them.

This is huge, so if you didn't grasp this concept stop now. Go back and read it again. This is all of the content you'll ever need for your website. As you continue to provide solutions, add more content.

http://wbp.bz/ww4ba

www.ingramcontent.com/pod-product-compliance
Lightning Source LLC
Chambersburg PA
CBHW071601210326
41597CB00019B/3347